I0764121

CHASE OF THE WALRUS.

SEASONS WITH THE SEA-HORSES;

OR,

SPORTING ADVENTURES IN THE NORTHERN SEAS.

BY JAMES LAMONT, ESQ., F.G.S.

"There we hunted the walrus, the narwal, and the seal.
Aha! 'twas a noble game,
And like the lightning's flame
Flew our harpoons of steel."—LONGFELLOW.

NEW YORK:
HARPER & BROTHERS, PUBLISHERS,
FRANKLIN SQUARE.
1861.

Dedication.

TO

SIR CHARLES LYELL, F.R.S., F.G.S., &c.

MY DEAR SIR CHARLES,

A copy of your delightful *Principles of Geology* has been my unvarying and instructive companion during ten years of adventurous wanderings, during which every thing I have seen seems to me entirely confirmatory of your geological views.

I therefore dedicate this little book to you; and I shall esteem myself fortunate if any of the observations contained in it shall be the means of riveting or strengthening a link in the beautiful chain of evidence by which you have in such a masterly manner demonstrated the perfect adequacy of *present causes* to remodel the surface of the earth. And with sincere respect I remain, my dear Sir Charles, yours very truly, JAMES LAMONT, F.G.S.

KNOCKDOW, ARGYLESHIRE.

CONTENTS.

CHAPTER I.

First Trip to Spitzbergen in 1858.—Find schooner Yacht and light Gigs unsuitable.—Determine to go again in 1859.—Hire a suitable Vessel and Crew, and build two Boats.—Lord David Kennedy agrees to accompany me.—Contested Election delays our starting.—Result of Poll unfortunate alike for Walruses and Constituency.—Preliminary Trip to Guernsey.—Sail from Leith.—Steamer a little out in her Reckoning.—Dreadful Famine in Lerwick.—Gale.—Namsen Fiord and River.—Salmon Fishing.—Terry's Breech-loading Rifles .... Page 17

CHAPTER II.

Hammerfest.—The "Anna Louisa."—Dr. de Jongh.—Norwegian Grouse.—Sail for Spitzbergen.—Shark Fishery.—Bear or Cherie Island.—Multitudes of Sea-fowl.—Sight Spitzbergen.—Post-office.—Wybe Jan's Water.—Meet the Ice.—Brig Nordby.—Captain Ericson.—Disastrous Spring-fishing.—Empress of India.—Loss of a Telescope and a Man's Life.—Boy-walrus.—Thick Ice.—Meet the Sloop, and sail in company to the East.—Shift our Flag, and send the Yacht to Bell Sound 28

CHAPTER III.

Preparations.—Description of a Walrus-boat, and Implements used.—Harpoons.—Lances.—The Haak-pick, or Seal-hook.—Axes.—Knives.—Ice-anchors.—Compass 43

CHAPTER IV.

Crow's-nest. — Look-out. — First Walrus seen. — Find them very shy.—Great Ice-pack.—Two Walruses shot.—Lay-to in a dense Fog.—Wreck of a Sloop in the Ice.—Cure for frost-bitten Feet.—Sketch of the Spitzbergen Walrus-hunter. — Profits of the Trade. — Truck System.—Cold.—Chilblains.—Seal-shooting on the Ice.—Method of hunting the Great Seal. — Dimensions of Great Seal. — Seal-shooting in the Water ....Page 52

CHAPTER V.

Hunting the Walrus.—Windfall.—Maternal Affection of Walrus.—Seal's Dinner.—Molluscæ.—Whale's Food.—Herd of Walruses.—Four killed.—Escape of a fine Bull.—Cutting up the Blubber.—Walrus Hide and Blubber.—Accommodations of "Anna Louisa."—"Whittling" a great Resource. —Vast Herds of Sea-horses.—"Jaging" them.—Exciting Sport.—Man killed by a Walrus.—Spitzbergen Gazette of June 16th.—Walrus Veal or Foal.................. 68

CHAPTER VI.

Sabbath Observance.—Rewarded for ditto.—Our first Bear seen.—Kill him.—Lose the Sloop.—Quantities of Eggs.—Drift-wood.—Comes from Siberia.—Can not be *in situ*.—Geology of Thousand Islands. — Red Snow. — Caused by Mute of Alca Alle.—Bear Battue, and its Consequences.—Deplorable Effects of smelling Brandy............... 87

CHAPTER VII.

Northeast Gale.—Bears' Grease.—Errors in the Charts.—Geology.—Limestone.—Coal.—Creation of subalpine Flats.—Deeva Bay.—"Fast" Ice.—Bear's Mode of catching Seals. —Whale's Bones.—Glen-Turritt.—Large Extent of fixed Ice.—Many Seals shot.—Become my own Harpooner.—Glacier with detached *Moraine*.................. 100

CHAPTER VIII.

Large Bear shot.—Adventures of an Opera-glass.—Size and Weight of Polar Bear.—Stories of Bears.—She-Bear and Cubs.—Break-up of the Fast Ice.—Kill the old Bear, and catch the Cubs alive. — Shocking case of filial Ingratitude ....Page 117

CHAPTER IX.

The Ice disperses.—Lose a Bear and Cub.—Pot 600 lbs. of Bears'-grease. — Skins. — Slow going. — Seals attracted by Whistling.—Glaciers on the Coast.—Noises from them.—Submarine Bank.—Shooting Walruses.—Walruses fighting. — Walrus Tusks. — Awkward Customer. — Ivory. — Story of Mermaids. — Osteological Peculiarity. — Cook loses his Watch.—Shoot a Bear.—Cold Bath................ 131

CHAPTER X.

Boat-race.—Visit. — Ingenious Harpoon. — Hippopotamus.—Phoca Vitulina, or Little Seal.—Phoca Hispida, or Jan Mayen Seal. — Dreadful Smell of Cargo. — Ferocity of young Bear. — Drift-ice. — Stones and Clay on Icebergs.—Warm Day.—Beautiful Caverns in the Ice.—Upset of an Iceberg. —Young Ice.—Noises from Glacier.—Crimping a Walrus. — Ivory Gulls. — See a Bear. — Curious Delusion. — Gulf Stream and Arctic Current.—Danger of getting embayed. —Narrow Escape 145

CHAPTER XI.

Dense and sudden Fog.—Our Hours and Habits.—Supplies run short.—Meet the Yacht.—Their bad Success in Sport.—Novel Bullet-mould. — Geological Specimens. — Part company again.—Medical Treatment of sick Men.—Water up. —News.—Old Acquaintance.—Gradual Extinction of the Walrus.—They are receding farther North.—Nova Zembla. —Illness of young Bear.—Attempt to escape.—Aged Bull-

Walrus.—His probable Reminiscences.—Coal and Fossils.—Commander Gillies' Land.—Northeast Spitzbergen.—Bear shot from the Deck of the Sloop .... Page 159

CHAPTER XII.

Walruses leave the Banks and go upon Land.—Vast Herds ashore.—Frightful Massacre.—Just Retribution.—Cargo of Bones.—Beautiful Day and sudden Change.—Early northern Voyagers.—Scoresby's Opinion.—Open Polar Basin a mere Chimera.—Dr. Kane.—North Pole.—Scheme for reaching the Pole.—Parry's Sledge Expedition, and why it failed.—Alexei Markhoff's Expedition, and his difficult Return 173

CHAPTER XIII.

Whales' Bones.—Rapid Elevation of the Land.—Early Whale-fishery.—Shallowing of the Sea.—Trench plowed by an Iceberg.—Last Day at the Sea-horses.—Successful Stalk and double Shot.—Lose two Harpoons.—Very bad Luck.—Difficulty of shooting Walruses.—Gale.—Wrecks in Spitzbergen.—Insurance.—Kill a White Whale.—Description of the same.—Sail to the Rendezvous 185

CHAPTER XIV.

Smeerenberg, or Blubber Town.—Agrémens of ditto.—Discovery of Spitzbergen.—Barentz.—Whale-fishery.—Attempts to colonize the Country, and to make it a penal Settlement.—They fail.—The West Indies *versus* Spitzbergen.—Russian Robinson Crusoes.—Wintering Establishment.—How conducted.—Awful Mortality.—Final Tragedy.—Death of eighteen Men from Scurvy and Hunger.—Ingenious Counter-irritant.—Russian Bath.—Cricket.—Boats sewed together.—Post-office.—Signs of Deer.—Kill three Geese with Ball.—Find the "Ginevra," and change into her.—Nautical Nimrods.—Amusing Walrus-hunt.—Gun bursts 199

CHAPTER XV.

Bitter Cold.—Reindeer-shooting.—Three right and left Shots. —Delight of the Sailors.—Black Fox.—Ponche à la Spitzberg.—Description of the Reindeer.—High Condition he attains.—Excellence of his Flesh.—His Ignorance of Man.—Anecdotes.—Fine Valley.—Unexplored Channel.—Near Heinlopen Straits.—Unjust Attack.—Marrow-bones.—Ice-borne Boulders.—Good "Bag."—Two singular Mountains. —Thymen's Straits.—Meritorious Deer.—Receipt for Kabobs.—Splendid deer Forest.—Rejoin the Sloop. Page 216

CHAPTER XVI.

Dead Walrus found.—Bears nearly escape, but are caught.—Gale and Ice.—Mynherr Holmengreen.—Presents *more Kaffirorum*.—Send home the Sloop.—Result of Ericson's eight Months' Voyage.—South Cape.—Sugar-loaf Mountain. —"Right Whales."—Parasitical Gulls.—Practical Joke.—Arctic Fauna.—Chain of Subsistence.—Divergence of White Bear from original Stock.—Probable Origin of the Walrus. —And of the Seal.—Of the Cetaceans.—Changes in the South African Antelopes, caused by Desiccation of that country 237

CHAPTER XVII.

Horn and Bell Sounds.—Ice Fiord.—Pickled Reindeer's Tongues.—Arctic Foxes.—Geology.—Raised Beaches.—Fossil Cannon-balls.—Awful Avalanche.—Begins to get dark at Night.—Reach Hammerfest.—Sell our Cargo.—Take Leave of our Crew.—Sail home.—Equinoctial Gales. —Leith.—"Glut" of Bears in the British Market.—Conclusion.—Game List 258

Appendix 271

ILLUSTRATIONS.

1. Chase of the Walrus........................*Frontispiece.*
2. The Author's Yacht, the "Ginevra"............ *Vignette.*
3. View on the River Namsen....................Page 25
4. Walruses on the Ice 73
5. Seal-shooting.................................... 113
6. She-Bear and Cubs 128
7. Reindeer-shooting 219
8. Group of Reindeer.............................. 260

MAP OF AUTHOR'S ROUTE ....*at the end.*

SEASONS WITH THE SEA-HORSES.

SPORTING ADVENTURES

IN THE

NORTHERN SEAS.

CHAPTER I.

First Trip to Spitzbergen in 1858.—Find schooner Yacht and light Gigs unsuitable.—Determine to go again in 1859.—Hire a suitable Vessel and Crew, and build two Boats.—Lord David Kennedy agrees to accompany me.—Contested Election delays our starting.—Result of Poll unfortunate alike for Walruses and Constituency.—Preliminary Trip to Guernsey.—Sail from Leith.—Steamer a little out in her Reckoning.—Dreadful Famine in Lerwick.—Gale.—Namsen Fiord and River.—Salmon Fishing.—Terry's Breech-loading Rifles.

In August, 1858, while cruising in my yacht the "Ginevra," of 142 tons, on the coast of Norway, I was induced, by the accounts I received of reindeer and other game to be met with in Spitzbergen, to make a trip across from Hammerfest to that country. It being late in the season before we got there, our stay was very short, and our sport was limited to killing a few reindeer, seals, and Brent

B

geese, and to assist in the harpooning of one or two walruses, in the boats of a sealing brig, which we fell in with among the ice. I, however, saw enough of Spitzbergen to convince me that wonderful sport, and of a most original description, was to be obtained there by any one who would go at the proper season, with a suitably equipped vessel and proper boats, manned by a crew of men accustomed to the ice and to the pursuit of the walrus and the seal.

Although I have the honor to append the letters F. G. S. to my name, I make no pretensions to the character of a scientific geologist, but I was also very much impressed with the interesting field Spitzbergen affords to a votary of that noble science, and particularly with the strong evidence to be met with in support of the theory of the gradual upheaval of the land in that remote part of the world, and I was anxious to investigate farther this interesting phenomenon.

I perceived on this occasion that nothing could be more utterly inapplicable for ice-navigation than a long fore-and-aft rigged schooner yacht, as in threading the intricate mazes of the ice there was no possibility of stopping her "way" to avoid collisions, as is done by backing the topsails of a square-rigged vessel, and her frail planking and thin copper were exposed to constant destruction from the ice. The dandified "ultramarine blue" painted gigs were also totally unsuited for the rough work of pushing in among the ice in pursuit of the seal and the walrus; indeed, it was very fortunate for us that we did not succeed in harpooning one of the latter mighty amphibiæ from the yacht's boats, for my subsequent experience of the strength and ferocity of these animals leads me to believe that he would infallibly have pulled us all to the bottom of the sea.

In the spring of 1859, therefore, I made up my mind to have another trip to Spitzbergen, and to go about it in a more systematic way; so, early in the season, I wrote to a gentleman in Hammerfest, who had been good enough to accompany me on my previous trip as an amateur pilot, requesting him to hire for me a small, stout "jagt,"* suitably planked, and provided with a square topsail and every thing requisite for a summer's campaign against the feræ naturæ of the arctic regions; and including casks to stow their blubber in, as I expected to be reimbursed for at least a part of the heavy outlay these preparations entailed by the proceeds of skins and oil. I also ordered two suitable whale- (or rather walrus-) boats to be constructed in Hammerfest, of a size slightly larger than those commonly used, so as to admit of an amateur sitting comfortably in the stern without his having necessarily to act as one of the boat's crew; and, finally, I desired my agent to engage two skillful

* A small sloop without a topmast, a rig very general among the Scandinavian coasters.

harpooners, and men enough to man the boats and navigate the "jagt"—English sailors being almost as useless as the boats for this description of work.

On mentioning my projected expedition to a friend, renowned as a sportsman with the rifle and the spear on the plains of India, and telling him of the sport I expected among the icebergs of the North, he at once agreed to join me, and entered with heart and purse into the arrangements; and here let me state that, during ten years I have spent in traveling in different parts of the world, I have never fallen in with a pleasanter and more useful companion, or a keener and a braver sportsman, than Lord David Kennedy.

When we were nearly ready to start, and I was superintending the outfitting of my yacht at Southampton, I was most unexpectedly requested by the Liberal party of a Scottish county to become their candidate in the general election about to take place; so, deeming it my duty to sacrifice my amusement to my country's good, I stayed the preparations for sea, and for the ten following days I was engaged in all the excitement of an electoral contest. The result, by a very narrow majority, proved unfortunate for the walruses, although perhaps the cynical reader may be disposed to add, "fortunate for the constituency," and I was once more at liberty to proceed on my intended voyage.

After a visit to Guernsey for the purpose of

laying in a supply of cold-repelling fluids, etc., I sent the yacht round to Leith, while I traveled north by land, as I am not the least ashamed to confess that I have a strong preference for land-traveling when it is practicable.

On May 31st the yacht arrived in Leith Roads, but a violent gale of east wind prevented us from sailing for several days; however, we got under way at daylight on the 6th of June; but the day being calm, we were only off the village of Elie, at the mouth of the Firth of Forth, at seven in the evening, so I landed to pay a visit to some relations living there whom I had not seen for several years, and to procure some small stores which the steward had forgotten, and which he declared were "indispensable."

On the 8th, during a dense fog, we were off Aberdeen by our dead-reckoning, and were nearly run down by a tug steamer, from the deck of which a voice hailed in a strong Northumbrian dialect, requesting to know "how far they might be from Shields." I never saw any people look more surprised than they did on being told "about 240 miles," as they had lost their way in the fog for two or three days, and imagined themselves to be still only a few miles from the mouth of the Tyne.

We beat through the middle of the Orkney Islands on the 9th, and on the 11th, finding the wind still desperately ahead, with a heavy sea, we thought it would entail no great loss of time to put into

Lerwick to replenish our stock of fresh meat and vegetables, which, as well as fish and butter, we imagined, in the innocence of our hearts, must abound here; but, to our great surprise and disgust, we found there was no market, and scarcely any thing eatable to be bought. Will it be believed that in a sea-port town of 3000 inhabitants, and so far advanced in civilization as to be lighted by gas, there was actually not a joint of fresh meat, a pound of fresh butter, nor even any fresh fish to be purchased? After much foraging we did succeed in obtaining some milk, some indifferent bread, and some stale eggs. I went into a chemist's shop to purchase some photographic chemicals, and upon my remarking to the worthy proprietor that Lerwick appeared to be suffering from famine at present, he replied, "Oh yes, sir, this time of year is what we call *the starvation months* here."

As I was unwilling to sacrifice a whole day by waiting until sheep could be got from the country, we went on board and prepared to set sail, when, just as the anchor was atrip, two boats pushed off from the shore in hot haste: one of these conveyed some fisher-boys, who had just taken a miraculous draught of eight herrings, the first of the season, as they told us. The other coble conveyed a hungry-looking two-year-old Leicester sheep, in custody of its proprietor, a neighboring farmer who had heard of our necessities.

The purchase of the sheep and the eight herrings

was negotiated in a very few minutes, and then, "shaking the dust from our feet" on this wretched, poverty-stricken village, we renewed our hammering against the N.E. wind outside. The wind hung in this direction, *i. e.*, straight in our teeth, until the 15th, when it increased to a gale, against which we could make no progress at all. We were by this time off the coast of Norway, and recognizing the mountains as being those lying about the mouth of the Namsen Fiord, I determined to get inside for shelter until the gale should abate; and I thought that as we appeared likely to have the Nor-Easter all the way, we might as well take the opportunity of replenishing our fresh water and fuel. We accordingly ran up this noble fiord, and at 8 A.M. on the 16th cast anchor in a beautiful little bay opposite to the gloomy precipices forming the island of Otteröe. Most extraordinary labyrinthian clusters of islands and rocks lay on each side of the entrance to this fiord, but the passage is wide and clear, and being plainly laid down in the excellent Norwegian government chart, we had no difficulty about finding our way in. I set the crew to gather firewood and fill the water tanks, while we took a walk to the top of a neighboring pine-clad mountain. The Norwegian summer was just commencing, and every thing looked extremely fresh and beautiful.

The celebrated Namsen River runs into the head of this fiord. This queen of rivers is well known to anglers as being the finest salmon stream in Norway, or perhaps in the world. In by-gone days I had myself passed two summers (one of them in company with a dear friend now gathered to his fathers) in salmon fishing in that splendid river, and recollections came thick upon me now of the pleasant hours passed in his society, and of the thirty and forty pounders which we hooked and captured in the gigantic pools and magnificent rushing streams of the Namsen.* The good fishing water is a considerable way up, and only extends for about twelve miles of the river, when the salmon are stopped by one of the finest waterfalls in the world, called by the natives "Fiskum Foss" (Anglicè, "the Salmon's Fall"). This twelve miles of water belongs to many small proprietors, and is divided into six fishing-stations, which for several years back have been regularly let on lease to British sportsmen.

While the crew were engaged in wooding and watering, we employed ourselves in trying some breech-loading rifles, known as "Terry's patent;" but, although I shot a "loom" (a large species of diver) at 100 yards' distance with one of these, we

* To show the wonderful sport to be met with on this river, I may state, that in the summer of 1854 I killed to my own rod, in thirty days' fishing, 83 salmon, weighing in all 1350 lbs.; and *the best sixty* averaging 20 lbs. each. And even this has been far exceeded by others, and particularly by the late Sir Charles Blois, who fished this river for many years.

VIEW ON THE RIVER NAMSEN.

both came to the conviction that as sporting weapons they were nearly worthless, and were infinitely more troublesome and difficult, both to load and to clean, than the common muzzle-loader. While looking at these rifles in the shop of the inventor and patentee, I had formed a high opinion of them, and the result only showed how difficult it is to form an accurate opinion of any fire-arms without the test of actual practice in the field. I may add, that the principle seems to me to be still more inapplicable to military weapons than to sporting ones, as the mechanism is far too complicated to stand wear and tear and rough usage. I dare say the authorities at the Horse-Guards have since found out this for themselves, as I understand a number of these breech-loaders, in the form of rifled carbines, were contracted for, for the cavalry.

The gale having abated, we sailed again on the morning of the 17th, but the wind continuing N.E. we had to beat the whole way north, and did not reach Hammerfest until the 23d.

CHAPTER II.

Hammerfest.—The "Anna Louisa."—Dr. de Jongh.—Norwegian Grouse.—Sail for Spitzbergen.—Shark Fishery.—Bear or Cherie Island.—Multitudes of Sea-fowl.—Sight Spitzbergen.—Post-office.—Wybe Jan's Water.—Meet the Ice.—Brig Nordby.—Captain Ericson.—Disastrous Spring-fishing.—Empress of India.—Loss of a Telescope and a Man's Life.—Boy-walrus.—Thick Ice.—Meet the Sloop, and sail in company to the East.—Shift our Flag, and send the Yacht to Bell Sound.

We dropped anchor opposite the British vice-consul's house, and had that worthy official on board to breakfast. He informed us that our "jagt" had been got ready and was waiting for us; the boats, however, still required to be finished off and painted. Several small vessels engaged in the seal and walrus fishery had gone to Spitzbergen more than a month ago, but nothing had been heard of them since their departure.

After breakfast, the gentleman to whom I had written about the preparations came on board, and in company with him we went to inspect the "jagt," boats, etc.

I had hitherto been undecided whether to leave the "Ginevra" at Hammerfest, or to take her also over to Spitzbergen, but the sight and smell of the cabin of the "Anna Louisa" at once decided me to stick to the schooner as long as possible.

The "Anna Louisa" was an extremely ugly, clumsy little tub of a sloop, of about 30 tons British measurement, and was rigged with a particularly ill-fitting mainsail, a staysail, a jib, and a small square topsail. She was high at the bow and the stern, and round in the bottom, and altogether looked as if the intention of her builder had been that she should make as much leeway as possible, and upset at the first opportunity. The latter fate I afterward learned had very nearly overtaken her the summer before, and her subsequent performances in making leeway did not at all belie her appearance. She had been engaged in a Spitzbergen trip the previous summer, and looked and smelled as if she had not been cleaned since, as the stench of the putrid walrus oil in and all over her was perfectly sickening.

Her crew consisted of a "skyppar" or captain, two men rated and paid as harpooners and mates, a cook, and eight other seamen. The captain, the two harpooners, and two of the others had been many times at Spitzbergen, and were considered good and experienced hands.

She was fully equipped with harpoons and lines, lances, seal-hooks, axes, blubber-knives, a large bundle of white pine sticks, in the rough (to be converted into oars and shafts for the lances and harpoons); casks for the blubber (at present full of water and small coals for ballast); salt for the skins; provisions for the crew, consisting of salt beef and pork, dried fish, butter, rye bread, peas, molasses, tea and coffee, etc., etc.

As the "Anna Louisa" had a small walrus boat belonging to her, independently of the two being built for us, we determined that, in order to save time, she should sail at once; so, after a little difficulty in collecting the crew, who seemed more inclined to the worship of Bacchus than that of Diana, we got her off, with a fair wind, on the 26th of June. We had previously arranged with the "skyppar" to rendezvous at a little bay on the southeast corner of Spitzbergen; and, if that should be unapproachable from ice, then at Bell Sound on the west coast.

We had to wait three days for the boats to be finished and painted, and, as may be supposed, we soon exhausted the resources of Hammerfest in the way of amusement. I believe the principal fact in connection with it is, that it is the northernmost town in the world, being in lat. 70° 42′ N., and long. 23° 35′ E., yet from the influence of the Gulf Stream the sea never freezes here. Although great masses of snow still lay on the hills, and even close down to the water's edge, the weather was extremely hot, and the musquitoes as numerous and annoying as I ever knew them in Africa or America.

There is a large, ugly, *barny-looking*, red-tiled, and yellow-ochre painted wooden cathedral, which looks, and I suppose *is*, big enough to contain the entire population of the place; the latter amounts to about 1300, who mostly live in miserable, rotten-looking wooden huts, although the consuls and some few of the principal merchants have excellent and well-built houses.

This was quite the busy season here, and a good deal of trade appeared to be going on, as the harbor was full of small Russian luggers and other coasting craft. This trade consists chiefly in the exportation of dried fish and walrus-skins to Archangel and the other ports on the White Sea; getting from thence, in return, rye meal, salt beef, tar, hemp, and cordage. They also export seal and walrus oil, fish oil, and seal-skins to Newcastle and Hamburg, in return for cutlery, hardware, stoneware, dry goods, etc.

Hammerfest, in addition to the honor of being the most northerly town in the world, may assuredly lay claim to another superlative, viz., that of being the most unsavory place in the universe. The immense quantity of cod, ling, and seythe or coalfish, which are caught on the coast of Finmarken, are cured without salt, being merely beheaded and gutted, and laid down on the rocks or hung up on hurdles to dry. There were a great many *acres* of fish undergoing this process in and around Hammerfest at the time of our visit, and the whole atmosphere was redolent of semi-putrid fish in consequence.

There are also several extensive *boileries* of seal and walrus blubber, and of fish-liver oil, and I am sure that, if the numerous fair sufferers in Europe and America who swallow their daily drams of "pale brown cod-liver oil" were only to see the enormous vats full of rotting seythe livers, and to smell the horrific exhalations from these boiling-houses, it would sadly diminish the profits of the far-famed Dr. De Jongh.

We took several walks in the mountains, and shot a few ducks, ptarmigans, and ripas for the table. I have shot many hundreds of these two last-named birds throughout Norway, and I have not the smallest doubt on my own mind that they are both identical in species with our Scottish ptarmigan and red grouse, being merely, as Mr. Darwin would say, "strongly-marked varieties," altered by geographical conditions, such as the greater cold and the necessity for the protection of a plumage more resembling the country they frequent.* I

* The ptarmigan is called in Scandinavia the "fiëld-ripa," or hill-grouse; and the grouse the "dal-ripa," literally "valley-grouse." The first frequents the high, rocky hills, and is nowhere very abundant; it seems to me *exactly* the same as the ptarmigan, or white grouse of the Scottish mountains. The dal-ripa inhabits the rocky islands and birch-covered hill-sides in great numbers, and, although nearly as gray as the ptarmigan, I have not the slightest doubt of his being the same bird as our Scottish red grouse, which he exactly resembles in his size, his voice, his flight, his habits, and every thing except his color.

have very little doubt that, if the dal-ripas were taken to Scotland, or the red grouse to Norway, a few generations would be sufficient to cause them to resemble exactly the variety existing in the country to which they were transferred.

On the evening of the 28th we got the new boats on board the yacht, having first deposited her frail Cowes gigs in a warehouse ashore, and at 1 A.M. on the 29th I turned the hands up to make sail for Spitzbergen. The wind was very light, and it was long before we got out of sight of the island of Soröen.

On the 30th we passed a small vessel engaged in the shark-fishery. This singular pursuit is carried on extensively in the seas lying between Finmarken and Bear Island, where the soundings vary from 100 to 150 fathoms, and the modus operandi is to anchor by long, light hempen cables at about that depth, and then put overboard their lines baited with seal's blubber. When they get a "nibble," they drag their victim *de profundis* by means of a windlass, and when he appears at the surface they farther secure him with harpoons, and dispatch him with spears and axes. The arctic shark (*Squalus Groenlandicus* or *Borealis*) is very large, and his liver, which is the sole object of his persecution, af-

---

A species of grouse or ptarmigan is also well known to inhabit Spitzbergen, but I never was fortunate enough to see one, although very anxious to procure a skin, as I believe a specimen does not exist in any of the museums of Europe.

fords nearly its own bulk of fine oil, amounting, I am told, sometimes to upward of a barrel. (*Quære*, does Dr. De Jongh know any thing of *Squalus Groenlandicus?*)

This little vessel appeared to have been pretty successful, as her sides were quite white and silvery from the sharks being dragged against them; and I confess the sight made us regret that my yacht's ground-tackle was neither long enough nor light enough to admit of our participating in the amusement.

When these men kill a shark, they have a curious practice of inflating its stomach with a bellows and tying the gullet, in order to make the carcass float, as, if it sank to the bottom, all the other sharks would devote their attentions to their defunct friend, to the neglect of the seal's blubber.

About two A.M. on the 1st of July we passed Bear or Cherie Island, so called, I presume, on the *lucus a non lucendo* principle, because it certainly produces neither bears nor cherries at the present day. I believe the real reasons for its nomenclature are, that some of the early Dutch navigators, on their way to China, once saw a bear here, and that an English expedition, sent out by Alderman Cherie, of London, afterward erroneously fancied that they were the discoverers of the island, and tried to supplant its original name by that of their patron. There is said to be plenty of good coal cropping out of a precipice on the island.

Although this was the third time that I have passed close by Bear Island, I had never yet actually been able to see it, as it is generally shrouded by impenetrable mist. One can, however, always tell when you approach it by the enormous quantities of gulls, puffins, guillemots, razor-bills, divers, etc., which use it as a sort of head-quarters and nursery, and afford to the mariner a perfect index to its proximity.*

The thermometer here fell to 36°, and a fresh gale of southwest wind sprang up, and carried us at the rate of eleven knots an hour until we sighted South Cape, the southernmost promontory of West Spitzbergen, at 1 A.M. on the 2d.

We had been steering rather to the west, so as to keep clear during the gale of the heavy drift-ice which our pilot expected to be lying off the southeast of the island, and we now had to alter our course to nearly due east, so as to reach the appointed rendezvous. We got there in the evening, and found the little harbor blocked up by heavy ice, which extended all along the coast. There was no appearance of the sloop, so we got out one of the boats and sent the pilot ashore with a letter, inclosed in a bottle, and addressed to Isaac the skyppar, saying we had been there, and would return in a few days.

* Bear Island is inaccurately laid down on the charts; its actual longitude being 19° east from Greenwich, and not 20° east, as the charts make it.

There are some old ruinous Russian huts on this promontory, one of which we made use of as a post-office by hanging the bottle up inside of it.

It was very difficult to get the boat through the ice along shore, and the whole country was covered with deep slushy snow; we saw nothing ashore but a few Brent geese and Eider ducks.

3d. Thinking the sloop had not yet reached Spitzbergen, I determined to sail up the great gulf or sound called "Stour Fiord" or "Wybe Jan's Water," to a place called "Thymen's Straits," about forty miles distant, in hopes of getting a few reindeer for provisions, as we were now subsisting on a bull, which, in the absence of any thing better, I had purchased in Hammerfest.

Hitherto the fiord had appeared quite clear of ice, except a little about the shore, but on sailing about twenty miles north we sighted a long, low, white line of ice, extending like a wall apparently right across the fiord; we thought at first that this was a sheet of fixed or "fast" ice, but on approaching it we discovered that it was drift ice, mostly in small pieces, and very open. We saw two small vessels, which we made out to be a brig and a sloop, or "jagt," at some distance among the ice. Thinking the sloop might either be our own, or be able to give us some intelligence of her, we sent a boat on board during a calm. They knew nothing of our sloop, and reported an indifferent "fishing" hitherto; no vessel that they knew of had killed more than thirty walruses; they themselves had twenty, with forty great seals and one bear; they also informed us that the north coast of Spitzbergen, which is usually considered the best hunting-ground, was this year impracticable on account of large quantities of ice being jammed against the coast at the northwest promontory, called Hakluyt's Headland.

On the 4th it was dead calm, and one of the most beautiful, bright, sunny days imaginable; it even felt quite warm, although the thermometer was only 50° in the shade. We got a boat out, and rowed for about six hours among the ice, looking for seals, but only saw three, all of whom managed to save their blubber.

On such a day as this, in these latitudes, one can see to immense distances with great distinctness, and hills which we know by reckoning and observation to be forty or fifty miles off, appear to the eye as if they were not more than ten or twelve. This is, doubtless, owing to a very dry atmosphere, and also to the great *flatness* of the globe so near the pole permitting a much larger horizon to be visible.

In the evening we had drifted close up to the brig before mentioned, and upon hailing her I was pleased to find her the "Nordbye," of Tonsberg, the same brig I had met last summer among the Thousand Islands, and whose master had initiated me into the exciting sport of harpooning the walrus. I recognized the portly form of Captain Ericson—very like a "stour cobbe," or large seal himself—on the deck, and requested him to come on board to dinner, an invitation with which he promptly complied. The "Nordbye" had left Tonsberg in the Christiania Fiord in February for the seal fishery in the great ice-field in the neighborhood of Jan Mayen's Island, and, having been unlucky there, had only lately come to Spitzbergen as a *dernier ressort*, in hopes of making up a cargo; she is an unwieldy tub of 200 tons, with five boats and twenty-four men, and is far too small for the northwestern fishery, as she is unable to hoist or turn over a dead whale; while, on the other hand, she is too big for the Spitzbergen seal and walrus fishery, as no one locality is generally able to employ five boats at a time, and his crew are consequently only half employed. Ericson told us that the spring fishery at Jan Mayen's had been very unsuccessful and very disastrous; many vessels had gone home "clean;" several Scotch and Norwegian vessels had been much damaged, and two or three totally lost; among others, the "Empress of India," a bran new iron screw whaler, from Peterhead, which had cost £20,000, had gone down bodily, the crew escaping with difficulty into a Norwegian brig belonging to the same port and same owners as the "Nordbye." Ericson expressed his decided conviction that iron vessels will "never do" for the northern whale fishery, as the excessive cold renders the iron brittle, and concussions with the ice are apt to start the rivets.

The "Nordbye" herself had undergone a terrible battering in that inclement season in those stormy seas, and had only captured about 300 small Jan Mayen seals, whereas 3000 would hardly have been remunerative. Poor Ericson was farther in great tribulation on account of having broken all his telescopes. The mate, a fine young fellow of twenty-two, only two days before had tumbled out of the "crow's-nest" at the main-top-gallant-masthead on to the deck, along with the last telescope, and had broken it to pieces. Upon farther inquiry, I ascertained that he had broken *his own neck* at the same time, and was picked up dead. To do my friend Ericson justice, I must acknowledge that he seemed to regret the loss of his poor young mate even more than that of the telescope, which he had accompanied in its descent, although the latter was quite invaluable and indispensable here, and not to be replaced nearer than Hammerfest for ten times its weight in gold. We had only three telescopes between us; but, after a slight inward struggle, I prevailed upon myself to present one of them to Ericson, and I was happy to be able to render such an important service to so good and obliging a fellow.

Before parting company, we went on board the "Nordbye" to see a young live walrus ("a leetle boy-walrus," as Ericson in his broken English called it), which they had on board as a pet. This interesting little animal was about the size of a sheep, and was the most comical fac-simile imaginable of an old walrus. He had been taken alive after the harpooning of his mother a few weeks ago, and now seemed perfectly healthy, and tame and playful as a kitten. It was, of course, a great pet with all on board, and seemed much more intelligent than I could have believed; the only thing which seemed to destroy its equanimity was pulling its whiskers, or pretending to use a "rope's end" to it, when it would sneak off, looking over its shoulder, just like a dog when chastised. They said it would eat salt fish, salt beef, blubber, or any thing offered it; but I strongly advised Ericson to give it, if possible, a mixture of vegetables or sea-weed along with such strong diet. I assured him that, if he succeeded in taking it alive to the Regent's Park or the Jardin des Plantes, he could get a long price for it; but before I left Spitzbergen, in September, I heard with regret that the curious little beast had died.

Ericson told me he did not think my yacht could penetrate to "Thymen's Straits" at present, as a great deal of ice intervened, and more continued drifting through the straits from the eastward; but as it looked tolerably open, I resolved to try. Upon penetrating a few miles in, however, we found it was impossible, and we therefore had to make up our minds to a continuance of the bull for the present.

We sailed down the fiord again on the 5th to look for our consort, or to see if she had left any letters for us at the post-office; on nearing the Russian huts we saw a small sloop, which hoisted the flag of Norway and Sweden, and which we soon made out to be the "Anna Louisa." She had been driven a good deal to the east during the gale on the 1st and 2d, and had not met with any great quantity of ice, except among the Thousand Islands; but several small vessels were hunting, or, as they call it, "fishing," to the eastward. Our men had only seen two walruses, but they had killed four seals, and these formed the commencement of a cargo which afterward swelled to goodly proportions.

Our people were of opinion that our best chance of sport lay to the northeast of the Thousand Islands, where there are extensive submarine banks, much affected by the walrus; but as we were very reluctant to exchange the comfortable cabins of the "Ginevra" for the narrow and odoriferous bunks of the "Anna Louisa," we decided on keeping in company as long as the ice would permit the former to get through; but, although we lowered the "Ginevra's" main-topsail, brailed up the foresail, and tacked up the mainsail, we had still some difficulty in keeping the yacht from running out of sight of her lubberly consort.

On the 6th we found the ice getting too thick for the "Ginevra," so we agreed to abandon her altogether, and to shift our flag into the "Anna Louisa" for good. We occupied about one half the day in transferring our guns, bedding, provisions, ammunition, etc., from the yacht to the sloop; we also took with us the yacht's cook and Lord David's servant James, which made up a total of sixteen souls for the sloop, leaving ten in the yacht; we took the two new walrus boats with us, and transferred the small old one to the yacht; we farther gave them a large cask, in which to stow the blubber of any seals they might get. I gave the sailing-master of the yacht instructions in writing "to proceed to Bell Sound, and there to kill as many reindeer as possible; if no reindeer were procurable, to cross again to Hammerfest for provisions, and in either case to be back without fail at the Russian huts on or before the 6th of August." I also instructed him to employ his personal leisure in collecting and carefully labeling fossils and shells, and also small bags of gravel from different elevations, as well as some specimens of whales' bones and drift-wood from the highest elevations he could find them on.

I appointed the mate to be *maître de chasse*, and intrusted him with one of the Terry's rifles and a single-barreled shot-gun, with lots of powder, shot, caps, and cartridges; we then parted company, and proceeded to make ourselves as comfortable as circumstances would admit of on board the sloop.

CHAPTER III.

Preparations.—Description of a Walrus-boat, and Implements used.—Harpoons.—Lances.—The Haak-pick, or Seal-hook. —Axes.—Knives.—Ice-anchors.—Compass.

THE crew are busy in shaping the rough white pine poles into oars, and shafts for the spears and harpoons, sharpening all the blades to a razor edge on a grindstone mounted on deck for the purpose, and otherwise fitting up the boats for immediate operations against the sea-horses.

I may as well here proceed to give a general description of the way in which this pursuit is conducted, as well as of the tackle and implements made use of, as it will enable the reader more clearly to understand my account of our own personal experiences afterward.

A well-constructed and well-appointed walrus-boat for five men is twenty-one feet long by five feet beam, having her main breadth about one third from the bow. She is *bow-shaped* at both ends, and should be at once strong, light, swift to row, and easily turned on her own centre; this latter quality is attained by having the keel a good deal depressed in the middle. She is always carvel-built, that construction of boat being much less liable to damage from the ice and the tusks of the walruses than a clinker-built boat, as well as much easier to repair if actually damaged; these boats have a very thick and strong stem-piece and stern-piece, to resist concussions with the ice. Each man rows with a pair of oars hung in grummets to stout single thole-pins: the steersman directs the boat by also rowing a pair of oars, but rowing with his face to the bow; and as there are six thwarts, each thirty inches apart, he can, if necessary, sit and row like the others. This mode of steering a boat has great advantages over either a rudder or a single steering oar as used by the whalers, for it not only turns the boat much quicker than either, but it economizes the entire strength of a man in propelling the boat. The advantage of each man rowing a pair of oars is, that the boat can be turned much quicker, and the oars, being short, are less in the way among ice. The harpooner always rows the bow oars, and is, of course, the commander of the boat; he alone uses the weapons and the telescope; the strongest man in the boat usually sits next to the harpooner, to hold and haul in the line when a walrus is struck, and it is also his duty to hand the harpoons and lances to the harpooner as required.

There is a deep notch cut in the centre of the stem-piece, and three others in a piece of hard wood on each side of it; these are for the lines running through, and great care is requisite to prevent them from slipping farther aft on the gunwale than the notches, as if they do the boat will probably be upset; it is from this cause that most of the accidents that one occasionally hears of occur.

There is sometimes also a "bollard," or little upright post, in the bow of the boat, for making fast the lines to, but many harpooners prefer to dispense with this, using instead the foremost thwart of the boat.

The boats are invariably painted white outside, in order to make their appearance assimilate as much as possible to that of the ice, and I think it would also be a great advantage to have the crews dressed in caps and jackets of some shiny white material, which would keep its color in spite of dirt and grease.

Each boat is usually provided with six harpoon heads, fitting, three on each side, inside of the bow, into little racks covered with curtains of painted canvas to prevent their sharp points and edges from being blunted or accidentally wounding the men. These harpoons are used indifferently for the seal and the walrus, and are, with all their apparent simplicity, the most perfect weapon that can be contrived for the purpose. When the instrument is thrust into the animal and his struggles draw tight the line, the larger outer barb takes up, as it were, a loop of his gutta percha-like hide or the tough reticulated fibres containing his blubber, while the smaller inner barb, like that of a fish-hook, prevents it from becoming disengaged. The best proof of its excellence is, that when a walrus is once properly harpooned and the line tight, he very rarely escapes. Each of these harpoon heads has *grummeted* round its neck one end of a line of twelve or fifteen fathoms long, each line being neatly coiled up in a separate flat box under the front thwart, and the opposite end secured to some strong part of the boat inside. The lines do not require to be longer, because the walrus is not generally found in water more than fifteen fathoms deep, and even if the water should happen to exceed that depth, he is not able to drag the boat under, from inability to exert his full strength when subjected to the pressure of twelve or fifteen fathoms of water. The lines are made of two-inch tarred hemp rope, *very soft laid*, and should be of the very finest materials and best possible workmanship.

There are generally four shafts for the harpoons, and it is not customary to keep more than one mounted, unless when walruses are actually in sight. They are made of white pine poles twelve or thirteen feet long, planed down to about an inch and a half or an inch and a quarter in thickness, and are tapered to a point for about four inches at one end to make them fit into the sockets of the heads. After placing a harpoon on a shaft, it is fixed by striking the butt end of the shaft smartly against a little block of wood, which is fixed for the purpose between two of the timbers of the boat, about fifteen feet from the bow, and on the starboard side.

The harpoons are used either for thrusting or darting, and a skillful harpooner will throw them with sufficient force to secure a walrus at four or five fathoms distance; when possible, however, they are always thrust or stabbed into the animal, and in that case it is customary to give the weapon a twist or wrench, both for the purpose of withdrawing the shaft, that it may not be lost or broken, as well as to entangle the barbs more securely in the walrus's skin or blubber. If this precaution is neglected, the harpoon may, perhaps, come out by the cut which it made on entering; this is more likely to happen if the intended victim be lying with his skin *slack*.

When there is much likelihood of falling in with white whales (*Beluga* or *Balæna albicans*), it is usual to carry one harpoon of a different construction, and with fifty fathoms of line attached, for their especial benefit. The reason for requiring a different harpoon for these cetaceans is, that their skin is not, like that of a walrus, the toughest part of their body; but the skin of *Balæna albicans*, on the contrary, is quite tender, gristly, and gelatinous, and the barbed iron, therefore, requires to be driven in until it secures good holding in his flesh beneath the blubber.

Next in the list of the boat's appurtenances come four or five enormous lances, with shafts as "large as a weaver's beam," but as neither I myself, nor probably my readers, have any notion of what a "weaver's beam" may be like, I will explain that the shaft is a white pine pole nine feet long and one and a half inch thick at the handle, increasing upward to two and a half inches thick where it goes into the socket of the iron. Formidable as this weapon is, the iron shank is very frequently bent double, or the stout shaft snapped like a twig by the furious struggles of an impaled walrus; so, to prevent the head being lost, it is attached to the shaft by a stout double thong of raw seal-skin, tied round the shank and nailed to the shaft for about three feet up. The reason for having the shaft so disproportionately large is, that there may be buoyancy enough to float the heavy iron spear if it should happen to fall into the water, or if a walrus, as often happens, should succeed in wrenching it out of the operator's hands by the violence of his contortions. I have once or twice had a boat's whole complement of lances rendered for the time unserviceable in the dispatching of a single walrus. The lances lie on the thwarts, with the blades protected in a box which is attached to the starboard end of the harpooner's, or foremost one.

The lance is not used for seals, as it is unnecessary, and spoils the skins, so that the *coup de grace* is administered to them by the "haak-pick" being struck into the brain. Each boat should have five of these implements, which are also indispensable as boat-hooks for pushing and hooking when the ice is too thick to allow of the oars being used.

There are then two axes, one a large one, used for decapitating the dead walruses, and the other, a small handy axe, which always lies close to the harpooner, is for cutting the line in case any thing goes wrong, or a walrus proves so fierce and mischievous that they may wish to be quit of him on any terms.

Five or six large sharp knives are for stripping the skin and blubber off the animals, or "flensing" them, as it is called in the fisher's parlance.

An ice-anchor is employed for anchoring the boat to an iceberg, and also to afford a *fulcrum* by which, with the help of two double-purchase blocks and twenty-four fathoms of rope (also forming part of every boat's appointments), five or even four men can drag the biggest walrus on to a moderately flat iceberg for the purpose of flensing him.

A small compass is indispensable, and ought to be fitted into a box attached below the seat in front of the steersman, after the fashion of a billiard-table chalk-box.

A telescope, a rifle, and plenty of ammunition, an iron bailing-ladle, also answering as a frying-pan, and a small copper kettle for making coffee.

There is a locker in the fore-peak, and another in the after-peak of the boat, and in these there ought to be always stowed a hammer, a pair of nail nippers, a small bag of nails, a piece of sheet lead for patching the boat if a walrus should put his tusks through her bottom, a bag of spare bullets, a canister of powder and caps, spare grummets, a box of matches and brimstone, a canister of coffee, and twenty or thirty pounds of rye bread. A mast, yard, and sail are taken if a stay of a few hours from the ship is contemplated; but a boat ought never to leave the ship's side without—or even to hang on the davits without—the whole of the other foregoing articles being inside of her; because, if a boat leaves the ship, even if only to kill a seal a quarter of a mile off, you never can be certain that you will not be ten or twenty days absent—nay, you never can be certain that you will ever see the ship again! You get led on and on insensibly, in the excitement of the chase, from one seal or one troop of walruses to another, and the awful dense fogs or sudden gales of these regions may come on and prevent your finding your way back.

In addition to all these absolute necessaries, we always had one luxury, consisting of a bag of mackintosh cloth lined with fur, and about seven feet by four, rolled into a tight bundle and strapped under the after thwart of each boat. This was to crawl into in case of being long out in severe weather; and, although we very seldom had occasion to make use of them, still the sense of comfort and security they gave one was very great, because I consider that they made one quite able to defy any cold that can occur, even in the Arctic regions, in summer. As for provisions, I never felt any uneasiness on that score, as, even if a seal or a walrus could not be immediately obtained, there were always plenty of eider ducks on the islands and outlying skerries; and the sea every where abounded with divers and guillemots, plenty enough and tame enough to be shot with a rifle. If a stay of many hours from the ship was contemplated, I generally took with me a shot-gun and a bag of shot for the purpose of killing fowls for food if necessary.

CHAPTER IV.

Crow's-nest. — Look-out. — First Walrus seen. — Find them very shy.—Great Ice-pack.—Two Walruses shot.—Lay-to in a dense Fog.—Wreck of a Sloop in the Ice.—Cure for frost-bitten Feet.—Sketch of the Spitzbergen Walrus-hunter. — Profits of the Trade. — Truck System.—Cold.—Chilblains.—Seal-shooting on the Ice.—Method of hunting the Great Seal. — Dimensions of Great Seal. — Seal-shooting in the Water.

In a brig like Ericson's there is always a "crow's-nest" (a contrivance in the shape of a cask, large enough for a man to get into, and made either of wood or canvas) fixed at the main-top-gallant-mast-head; but in a small vessel such as we had, the look-out man simply sits on the main gaff or the topsail yard. From our topsail yard, with a good telescope, we could see a single seal on white ice in a clear day about four miles off, and from a crow's-nest as high as Ericson's I believe about double that distance—a prodigious advantage for the larger vessel. As may be supposed, it is rather a cold position than otherwise, that on the topsail yard, and the men, not unnaturally, are apt to neglect this all-important duty; but, in sailing within sight of ice, a careful man, with a telescope, ought to be constantly there, because, if the ice is rough, even a large herd of walruses may be in sight one minute and concealed by high intervening icebergs the next. The look-out man, of course, requires to be relieved very frequently.

Shortly after parting with the yacht, our look-out man reported "walruses on the ice," and we had each several chances the same day; but the walruses were all old bulls, in small troops of two, three, or four, and so extremely shy that we could not get near enough to harpoon them, and we were advised by the people to refrain from firing at them, as they have a theory that it is almost impossible to shoot a walrus dead, and that it also frightens them and renders them wilder than ever. There is no doubt as to its making them wild; but we soon found out that, when a walrus was wild already, the only chance of bringing him to bag was by firing at his head. At first, however, we failed to do much execution, because, at the advice of the harpooners, we waited until all chance of harpooning the walruses was at an end; and then, when they were all scuffling pell-mell into the water, accurate shooting became next to impossible. Our want of success at first was also partly attributable to not understanding the anatomy of the animal, and hence imagining that his brain lay in what appears to be his head, but which is actually only the bony process supporting the tusks; the brain, in reality, lies far back, and the back part of the head is completely buried in the folds of fat or blubber surrounding the neck.

On the 7th the weather continued foggy, with a cold northeast wind, and we made very little progress against it. We are coasting along the outside of this great ice-pack, which fills up Deeva Bay, and embraces the whole archipelago of the Thousand Islands. This, the east side of the pack, has its edge clear and well-defined, being packed tight by the joint influence of the northeast wind lately prevailing and the current, which always sets more or less in the same direction. When going in pursuit of the walruses among the ice, it is sometimes very difficult to get the boats through the ice at the outer edge of the pack, where it is so closely wedged together, and we generally have to drag them over the ice with great labor for fifty or sixty yards, until we get into opener water inside the pack. This morning Lord David shot a cow walrus through the head as she was shuffling off the ice. She immediately sank, but floated up again in a few seconds, when she was harpooned and secured.

In the afternoon I went after another cow, which, with two half-grown young ones, lay apparently asleep on a small outlying patch of icebergs. As usual, we got *almost* near enough to harpoon them, when the old one got alert, and immediately aroused the two young ones, and, as they seemed unwilling to move, she rolled them one after the other like barrels into the water, and was in the act of following them herself, when my rifle bullet penetrated her brain, and she tumbled head foremost off the iceberg, and instantly sank to appear no more. The two young ones came up again and again, as if looking for their dam, but would not allow us to approach them.

The people say that the walruses about this part must have been very much hunted, as they are so shy; but they encourage us by saying that, when we get farther to the northeast, we shall find plenty of more unsophisticated individuals, who will allow themselves to be harpooned.

On the morning of the 8th we got past the end of the pack, and got a glimpse through the thick fog of "Black Point," a gloomy promontory, forming the southeast corner of Edge's Land, as this division of Spitzbergen is called. Nothing was visible ashore but snow, with desolate-looking patches of bare brown earth peeping through it here and there, or the bare rocks on some "wind-loved" peak from which the snow had been blown.

About midday the fog got thicker, and we found ourselves running in among some heavy icebergs; so, as we did not know what the ice ahead might be like, our prudent skyppar judged it advisable to lay-to and wait for clearer weather.

The greater part of the eastern coast of Spitzbergen is covered with a succession of enormous glaciers, descending down to the water's edge, and even protruding far into it. I imagine that these prodigious masses of ice generate the fogs, which it is notorious are much more prevalent here than on the west side of the country.

9th. The fog is not quite so thick, but a very cold wind is blowing from the northeast, and the thermometer on deck is just above freezing-point. In such weather seals and walruses do not lie on the ice, nor show more than their heads above water occasionally, as if to inquire if the weather above was getting any more favorable for basking. We pretty much imitate these sensible amphibia in our habits, as we don't show much on deck.

In the afternoon a small sloop came in sight, and appeared desirous of speaking us, so we hove-to for them. The captain of the sloop then came on board in a boat, and, touching his cap to us, he began a dismal story, which my slight knowledge of Norsk did not enable me to follow, so we had it translated to us by one of our crew, who, from having sailed in an American ship to San Francisco, could speak tolerable English, or rather *American.* It appeared that about three weeks ago another small sloop, with a crew of six men, had been totally lost among the ice near Hope Island. The crew had taken to their boat, and had been rowing and drifting about, looking for another vessel, until yesterday, when this sloop had picked them up. They were in the last extremity from cold and hunger, having had nothing to eat for several days past but the dry seal-skin mufflings of their oars—two of them, who were in this boat, looked very thin and pale. The worst of the story was that the captain of the wrecked vessel had got both his feet badly frost-bitten, and the object of this other skyppar in now visiting us was to ask if we were going over to Hammerfest soon, that we might take the poor man with us, or if we had any medicine with us which would cure him. We had no medicine but a box of pills and one of Seidlitz powders, and doubting the efficacy of these in a case of mortification, I recommended them to take the man over to Norway immediately, or else to amputate the frost-bitten parts of his feet without farther delay. The master of the sloop replied that he and his crew could not afford to sacrifice their summer's profits by leaving the ice with their vessel only half full, and were afraid to take upon themselves the responsibility of performing the amputation. I then told them them that, as we had just come out, and had already the same number of souls on board our smaller vessel as they had, with the addition of the six castaways, we did not feel that it was incumbent upon us either to go over to Norway or to relieve them of the charge of any of the men. I remembered hearing long ago, in the case of a friend who had shot his arm off, that bandages wet with port wine were applied to keep off mortification, and so, as the nearest approach to that stimulant in our possession, we gave them a couple of bottles of rum, and advised them to apply that either externally or internally, as they might deem most advisable.

We heard a few days afterward that by great

good luck they had fallen in with a small schooner belonging to the same owners as the wrecked sloop, and that this schooner, having her cargo nearly completed, had taken the six men over to Hammerfest; and I afterward ascertained, upon our return to Norway, that the poor captain's life had been saved, but by the terrible alternative of amputating the greater part of both his feet.

It is a terribly hard and dangerous life these Spitzbergen walrus-hunters live, and I observe that they all have a restless, weary look about the eyes —a look as if contracted by being perpetually in the presence of danger. They are a wild, rough, reckless lot of fellows; bold, hardy, and enduring of cold, hunger, and fatigue; active and energetic while at sea, and nearly always drunk while at home. So many bad accidents have been caused by their having brandy on board, that of late the owners have supplied them with tea and coffee instead, and it is found that men work quite as well, and stand the climate quite as well, upon these as upon spirits; but this enforced temperance seems to cause a sort of reaction whenever they get the opportunity of indulging to excess.

Of late years the merchants of Tromsöe and Hammerfest, who fit out these vessels, have adopted the sagacious system of paying their crews by a share of the proceeds in lieu of money wages, and this, of course, is a very great stimulus to the men to work hard and to lose no opportunity of killing every walrus and seal that they possibly can. The usual system I believe to be as follows: The owners fit out and provision the vessel, and advance to the men on credit what money they require to buy clothing and to provide necessaries for their families during their absence: whatever the cargo obtained may consist of, one third of the gross proceeds is then set apart for the crew, and divided into shares, of which the captain gets three, each harpooner two, and the other men one each. Thus, if the gross proceeds of a voyage in skins, blubber, and ivory be estimated at $2000, and the number of hands amounts to ten, which is the usual number for a vessel with two boats, the shares will be worth $47½, or about £10 each; £10 is a much more important sum of money in Norway than it is in Britain; and so (putting aside the exciting nature of the occupation) it is not suprising that the best seamen and boldest spirits of the north of Norway should be generally found in the Spitzbergen sealers. These are the true descendants and successors of the gallant Vikings and Berserkars, who of old ravaged and conquered the coasts of Europe from Jutland to Otranto. This pursuit to these men has all the excitement of a lottery, because, in the case of a very successful season, they *may* make a good deal more than the above-stated amounts, and I dare say a good deal of the spirit of the gambler enters into their calculations. They are always over head and ears in debt to the merchants before they start, and so I believe it is usual for the owners to compound with the crew for the third of the cargo belonging to them by giving them a certain sum per walrus and per seal whenever they arrive, and as the poor ignorant men know nothing of the price-current of seal-oil, etc., in the markets of Hamburg or Bremen, and are naturally anxious to "realize" at once, I am afraid they are generally induced or intimidated into parting with their share of the hard-earned spoil at far below its market value. In fact, the "truck system" in all its iniquity prevails.

Our own crew, having been engaged so late in the summer as to render it unlikely that we should be able to get a full cargo, and also with the view of rendering them more entirely dependent on our wishes, were not engaged on this system, but got instead money wages at double the rate usual in Norway. This double pay was about equal in amount to that of the English sailors in my yacht.

I shot a large seal in the evening.

10*th*, *Sunday*. Thick, cold, raw fog all day; ropes all incrusted with ice, which falls down clattering on the deck every time any thing shakes. I begin to suffer a good deal from chilblains on the feet, an ailment I have not been addicted to since I was a schoolboy, *ætat.* eleven. This is perhaps not altogether to be wondered at, as the thermometer in our cabin ranges between 36° and 44°, and we sit in our fur great-coats and fur boots in order to avoid having the stove lighted, for we both think that in such a small confined place any cold is preferable to the heat and unwholesome closeness of a stove.

The 11th was just such another day, and we did not see twenty yards from the deck all day. In the evening a big seal was observed looming through the fog, and looking as large as a walrus in the haze. Lord David shot him dead. When a single animal is observed from the ship, we take it in turns to go after him, and as we always sleep in our clothes, we are ready at a moment's notice, at any hour of the day or night, whenever the watch on deck report any thing in sight. Our crew are divided into three watches of four hours each, but all hands are summoned on deck whenever a herd of walruses is seen, and, in case of both boats leaving the vessel, Isaac the skyppar and the ship's cook take charge on deck. Isaac himself is a renowned harpooner, and a first-rate man altogether, but, unfortunately, he broke his left arm a few weeks before we sailed, so that he is unable to use the oar or the harpoon as yet. He makes a most excellent and careful ship-keeper, and we never have any uneasiness about being lost while we know that he is on deck. It must be rather dull work for him, being on deck alone for whole days, with the topsail aback, while the boats are miles out of sight in the ice. We have ordered him to hoist the flag if he should see a bear or a herd of walruses while we are absent, as, although the boats may not be visible from the deck, we can generally, as long as it is clear, see the sails of the sloop above the horizon.

It cleared up about midnight for a brief interval, and enabled us to get a beautiful view of the coast, with its enormous glaciers sweeping out into the sea in great semicircular arcs. There was plenty of ice all round, but in very open order. Ryk Yse Islands were visible to the north, among much heavy ice, which seemed to be fixed around them. We saw a small sloop several miles distant, and a large seal asleep on an iceberg, about equidistant from the other sloop and ourselves. Lord David went in pursuit of it; but we perceived from the deck that the steersman had lost the bearings of the seal, and was steering in a wrong direction. For fear the other sloop should be before us, we then hastily lowered my boat and rowed straight to the seal. On nearing the phoca, he appeared quite awake, and was looking nervously about him every two or three minutes, so we rowed round so as to get between him and the sun, which, although it was exactly midnight, was high and bright in the heavens. This dazzled his eyes so completely, that, although he was wide awake, and looked straight in our direction repeatedly, he could see nothing for the glare, and he lay still until the boat approached to within about fifty yards, when my bullet perforated his cerebellum, and he sank motionless on the ice.

The pursuit of the great Spitzbergen seal (*Phoca*

barbata), although it lacks the wild excitement of the chase of the sea-horse, is a very delightful amusement. The great seal will never allow himself to be "caught napping." I do not think I ever saw a sleeping seal which did not, about once in every three or four minutes, raise his head from the ice and look uneasily around; so that he can not be harpooned in his sleep, like his more lethargic congener the walrus. I imagine this greater watchfulness on the part of the seals to arise from the greater cause they have to apprehend being "stalked" by the bears while taking their siesta; however this may be, recourse *must* be had to the rifle before the harpoon comes into play in the case of *Phoca barbata*, and to make good work with them requires the perfection of rifle-practice, for if a seal be not shot stone dead on the ice, he is almost certain to roll or jerk himself into the water, and sink or escape; and as a seal never lies more than twelve inches from the edge of the ice, the most trifling spark of life is enough. The only part of the huge carcass in which a bullet will cause the requisite amount of "sudden death" is the brain, and this, in the biggest seal, is not larger than an orange. A seal will seldom allow the boat to approach nearer than fifty or sixty yards, and a large proportion take the alarm much sooner. Every rifle volunteer and every gunmaker's apprentice who reads this will probably exclaim, "Oh, there is no difficulty in that; I can hit an orange every shot at

100 yards!" This may be true, my gallant volunteer or skillful gunmaker, but you have not yet taken into account that the boat is heaving more or less from the motion of the waves, and that the slab of ice on which your orange is lying is heaving also; and this, upon consideration, you will admit increases the "difficulty" a little; neither Lord David Kennedy nor myself were altogether tyros in the use of the rifle before we began, but we found the difficulty considerable; however, after a few days we became adepts at it, and rarely missed killing a seal dead. The rifles we both used were elliptical, four-barreled Lancaster's of 40-gauge. During the last 100 or 150 yards of the boat's approach to the seal, the steersman alone propels it by gently paddling it with two oars, one eye on the seal and the other on his oars; if the seal looks in the direction of the boat, he stops rowing, and great care is requisite on his part to avoid coming against pieces of ice, which make a *rasping* noise, almost sure to attract the attention of the seal. I need hardly observe that the boat must also keep carefully to leeward, as the seal has an acute sense of smell; and if the advantage of the sun can be obtained in addition, as in the case above related, the moments of *Phoca barbata* are probably numbered. I always knelt in the bow of the boat, and selected my own opportunity to fire, and, the moment the rifle was discharged, all the men rowed with their utmost strength to the spot, where, if the seal showed any

symptoms of life, I always darted a harpoon into him; but, if he seemed quite dead, some one jumped out and struck the haak-pick into his head, and dragged him away from the edge for fear he should come alive again. This is not an unnecessary precaution, as I have known a seal, apparently stone dead, give a convulsive kick over the brink of the ice, and go to the bottom like a sixty-eight pound shot, while his proprietors, as they delusively considered themselves, were standing within two feet of him.

When the seal is fairly dead, all the men except one get on the ice, and with their knives they strip the skin and blubber, in one sheet, off his body in a very few minutes. The carcass, or "krop," is then thrown into the sea, that it may not be mistaken for a live seal at a distance; the blubber is laid flat in the bottom of the boat, and you proceed in quest of more or return to the ship.

A full-sized Spitzbergen seal, in good condition, is about nine and a half or ten feet long, by six or six and a half feet in circumference, and weighs six hundred pounds or upward. The skin and fat amount to about one half the total weight. The blubber lies in one layer of two or three inches thick underneath the skin, and yields about one half of its own weight of fine oil. The value of a seal of course varies with the state of the oil market all over the world; but, at the time of which I write, oil being unusually cheap, they only averaged about five or six dollars apiece; but still the fact of the animals being of some use contributed to render the chase of them much more exciting, as nothing can be more distasteful or unsatisfactory to the feelings of a true sportsman than taking the life of any thing which is to be of no use when dead.

When seals are *in the water* they are not the least afraid of a boat, but come boldly up quite close to it, first on one side and then on the other, as if impressed with the deepest curiosity to see what the unusual-looking object is. When they are shot dead in the water, however, they sink so rapidly that it is very difficult to get possession of them. The most approved plan is not to fire unless the boat's head is directed toward the seal and distant not more than thirty yards; then, if the men all give way instantly and vigorously, you *may* be in time to thrust or dart the harpoon into the seal before he sinks, but more likely you will only be in time to see him sinking far down in the clear water with his tail downward. Some people compute that "one half of the seals shot in the water, even with skillful management, are lost;" others say "two thirds;" and, from our own experience, I am inclined to think it is two to one on the seal, or thereabouts. I have several times lost six consecutively, and a most tantalizing proceeding it was; but, bad luck as that may seem, it is nothing; for our head harpooner, Christian, a very smart fellow, told me that one day he shot dead eighteen immense seals, and lost every one of them! If you merely *wound* a seal in the water, there is a much better chance of getting him than if he is killed outright, as he sometimes flounders on the surface till he is harpooned. I have often thought that it would answer to use small shot when they come so close. and I regret never having made the experiment.

CHAPTER V.

Hunting the Walrus.—Windfall.—Maternal Affection of Walrus.—Seal's Dinner.—Molluscæ.—Whale's Food.—Herd of Walruses.—Four killed.—Escape of a fine Bull.—Cutting up the Blubber.—Walrus Hide and Blubber.—Accommodations of "Anna Louisa."—"Whittling" a great Resource.—Vast Herds of Sea-horses.—"Jaging" them.—Exciting Sport.—Man killed by a Walrus.—Spitzbergen Gazette of June 16th.—Walrus Veal or Foal.

The fog was as thick as ever again on the morning of the 12th, and we were tantalized by hearing the snorting and bellowing of a great many walruses in the immediate vicinity, although we could not find them for the fog; but it fortunately cleared up for a little in the forenoon, and enabled us to see a great herd of walruses reposing on several large flat slabs of ice. We instantly went after them in both boats, and, although they were very shy, we each succeeded in killing a cow and a calf. The cow killed from my boat had a good harpoon and line sticking in her back; it had not been long in the walrus, and appeared to have been lost by the slipping of the knot at the inner end of the line. According to the laws of the ice, both walrus and tackle—even if the former had been dead—were a fair prize of the captors, although Christian said he knew very well to whom the harpoon had belonged.

I never in my life witnessed any thing more interesting and more affecting than the wonderful maternal affection displayed by this poor walrus. After she was fast to the harpoon and was dragging the boat furiously among the icebergs, I was going to shoot her through the head that we might have time to follow the others; but Christian called to me not to shoot, as she had a "junger" with her. Although I did not understand his object, I reserved my fire, and upon looking closely at the walrus when she came up to breathe, I then perceived that she held a very young calf under her right arm, and I saw that he wanted to harpoon it; but whenever he poised the weapon to throw, the old cow seemed to watch the direction of it, and interposed her own body, and she seemed to receive with pleasure several harpoons which were intended for the young one. At last a well-aimed dart struck the calf, and we then shortened up the lines attached to the cow and finished her with the lances. Christian now had time and breath to explain to me why he was so anxious to secure the calf, and he proceeded to give me a practical illustration of his meaning by gently "stirring up" the unfortunate junger with the butt end of a harpoon shaft. This caused the poor little animal to emit a peculiar, plaintive, grunting cry, eminently expressive of alarm and of a desire for assistance, and

Christian said it would bring all the herd round about the boat immediately. Unfortunately, however, we had been so long in getting hold of our poor little decoy duck that the others had all gone out of hearing, and they abandoned their young relative to his fate, which quickly overtook him in the shape of a lance thrust from the remorseless Christian.

I don't think I shall ever forget the faces of the old walrus and her calf as they looked back at the boat! The countenance of the young one, so expressive of abject terror, and yet of confidence in its mother's power of protecting it, as it swam along under her wing; and the old cow's face showing such reckless defiance for all that we could do to herself, and yet such terrible anxiety as to the safety of her calf!

This plan of getting hold of a junger and making him grunt to attract the others is a well-known "dodge" among the hunters; and, although it was not rewarded on this occasion, I have several times seen it meet with the full measure of success due to its humanity and ingenuity.

I opened the stomach of a seal of aldermanic proportions, who looked as if he had lately been attending a civic feast, and found in it, not turtle, but about a bushel of beautiful prawns, evidently just swallowed, and so fresh that we might have re-eaten them ourselves but for an unworthy prejudice. How animal life must swarm in these cold seas to maintain such a multitude of voracious animals! The keeper of the "Talking Seal" in London told me that they "gave her fifty pounds of fish a day, and that she *would eat* one hundred pounds if she could get it;" so we can form some idea of what the thousands of seals here must devour. The basis of all this gormandizing is undoubtedly the Medusæ or Jelly-fish, which in places are so numerous as actually to thicken and discolor the sea! Conspicuous among these are the small black animalculæ, popularly known to the Norwegian frequenters of these regions as "Hval-spise" or "Whales' food" (*Clio borealis*).

This singular mollusk may be briefly described as nearly resembling the body of a tadpole, but instead of the tail of the latter it is provided with a pair of wings like those of a bird, with which it propels itself through the water by a sort of flying motion. The sea is literally blackened in some places by the swarms of these animalculæ to such an extent that I have no difficulty in believing that the huge Mysticetus, with his enormous open mouth and whalebone brushes, may ingulf a sufficiency of them to maintain him. I collected a lot of these winged tadpoles, intending to preserve them in spirits of wine, but somehow that fluid reduced them in a few days to a sort of opaque pulpy mass. While they were waiting in a tumbler for a pickle-bottle to be cleaned and filled with spirits of wine for their reception, they fought furiously in a sort of indiscriminate *melée* among themselves, and were more particularly virulent against a small pink Jelly-fish which I put into the tumbler beside them.

13*th*. At 3 A.M. this morning we were aroused by the cheering cry of "Hvalruus paa Ysen" (walruses on the ice). We both got up immediately, and from the deck a curious and exciting spectacle met our admiring gaze. Four large flat icebergs were so densely packed with walruses that they were sunk almost awash with the water, and had the appearance of being solid *islands of walrus!*

The monsters lay with their heads reclining on one another's backs and sterns, just as I have seen rhinoceroses lying asleep in the African forests; or, to use a more familiar simile, like a lot of fat hogs in a British straw-yard. I should think there were about eighty or one hundred on the ice, and many more swam grunting and spouting around, and tried to clamber up among their friends, who, like surly people in a full omnibus, grunted at them angrily, as if to say, "Confound you, don't you see that we are full?" There were plenty more good flat icebergs about, but they always seem to like being packed as closely as possible for mutual warmth. These four islands were several hundred yards apart, and, after feasting our eyes for a little on the glorious sight, we resolved to take them in succession, and not to fire at first; but the walruses had not been long enough on the ice to have got

WALRUSES ON THE ICE.

properly sleepy, and the discontented individuals in the water gave the rest the alarm, so that we only managed to secure four altogether.

Solomon, our untried harpooner, acquitted himself pretty tolerably on this his first fair trial, for he killed one out of the first herd, and two at a time out of the second, but on the latter occasion he as nearly as possible upset the boat by allowing one of the lines to run over the gunwale aft of the notches at the bow: the boat most certainly would have been upset had it not been that it was ballasted with the blubber of the one already killed; as it was, she was half filled with water, and Lord David and the crew were on the point of jumping out, when fortunately she righted again.

This herd consisted chiefly of cows and young bulls, and they then dispersed or got out of reach among the ice.

In the forenoon we discovered a huge bull, with fine tusks, by himself sound asleep on a small sloping piece of ice, and I went in Solomon's boat to attack him. The shape of the iceberg would not permit us to approach within stabbing distance of the bull, but as he was not more than five yards from the bow of the boat, I very foolishly did not fire, as I considered the harpoon a certainty; but, to my utter disgust and astonishment, Solomon threw two harpoons one after the other, and missed the huge animal with both; the walrus awoke at the sound the second harpoon made on the ice, and was into the sea like a shot. The rest of the boat's crew were as much annoyed as myself, and anathematized the unhappy Solomon in every language spoken in Scandinavia. I believe I added some strongish expressions in English. We made up our minds to disrate Solomon if this occurs again, and to try another of the crew as harpooner instead of him.

14th. Northeast wind, thick fog, and hard frost, all the rigging incased with icicles. Hitherto all our skins, with the blubber attached, had been thrown into the hold "in bulk," but they have now accumulated so as to render it necessary that the blubber should be divided from the skins and stowed in the casks; we therefore take advantage of the fog to-day to perform this necessary but unpleasant process, which is conducted as follows:

There is set up across the deck, immediately aft the hatchway, a sort of frame or stage of stout planks, about four feet high, and sloping down at an angle of about 60° with the deck at the forward side. It is perpendicular aft, and at that side of it the two men who are to act as "specksioneers" (blubber-cutters) take their stand, clad in oilskin from top to toe, and armed with large knives, sharp as razors, and curved on the edge. The skins are then hoisted out of the hold and hung across the frame, two at a time, with the blubber side upmost. It is an operation requiring great dexterity to separate the fat from the skin, so as to remove the whole of it, and not to cut or shave the skin itself; but, by a sort of *mowing* motion of the knife, which is held in both hands, from left to right, these men do it with great rapidity and neatness. As the blubber is peeled off it is divided into slabs of twenty or thirty pounds' weight each, and thrown down the hatchway, where two men are ready to receive it, and to slip it into the square bung-holes of the casks; from its oleaginousness it soon finds its own level in the casks, and when full these are fastened up. I ought to have mentioned that the skins of full-grown walruses are always taken off the animal in two halves, being divided longitudinally down the back and the belly; the skins of calf walruses and seals are always left entire. Walrus hide is a valuable commodity, and sells for from two to four dollars per half skin, calves only counting for a half; it is principally exported to Russia and Sweden, where it is used to manufacture harness and sole leather; it is also twisted into tiller-ropes, and is used for protecting the rigging of ships from chafing. In former times nearly all the rigging of vessels on the north coasts of Norway and Russia used to be composed of walrus-skin.

When there is a superfluity of the article in the market I believe it is boiled into glue. It is from an inch to an inch and a half thick, very pliable in its green state, but slightly spongy, so that I should doubt the quality of the leather made from it.

The seal-skins mostly find their way to Scotland,

where, I believe, they are made into what are known in the hosiers' shops as "dog-skin" and "Dundee kid" gloves. Their value in Hammerfest is from one to two dollars a skin.

The walrus has not nearly so much blubber, in proportion to his size, as the seal; thus a seal of 600 lbs. will carry 200 or 250 lbs. of fat; an ordinary walrus may weigh 2000 lbs., but his fat will not exceed that of the seal. A full-sized old bull walrus must weigh at least 3000 lbs., and such a walrus will produce, if very fat, 650 lbs. of blubber, but seldom more than 500 lbs., which latter was, I think, about the maximum quantity yielded by the most obese of our victims. Neither does the fat of the walrus afford so fine an oil as that of the seal; but it is usual to mix them indiscriminately together, and the compound is always exported into Southern Europe under the name of seal oil.

We begin to find some of these long, dreary, foggy days intolerably irksome, as our cabin is singularly ill adapted for passing much idle time in. It is literally almost impossible either to sit, stand up, or lie down in it. It is only five feet high, except where a small dingy skylight three feet square gives us the advantage of another foot. There is a "bunk" on each side of about $5\frac{1}{2} \times 2\frac{1}{2}$, and one can hardly be said to be *lying down* in five and a half feet length; each bunk has a locker in front of it nine inches broad; and any one unfortunate enough to have to try will find that any posture is preferable to *sitting* long on a locker nine inches in breadth, with a perpendicular back. The cabin, from end to end, between these lockers, is about 7×4, but nearly half of this length is occupied by the angular projections forming the counter of the vessel, over which is the table, so that the space available for moving about, washing and dressing, etc., is exactly four feet square. Behind the after end of each bunk is a small open space filled by a barrel of biscuits, jar of butter, canisters of tea, coffee, and sugar, magazine of powder, bags of shot, etc., etc. Our guns, pouches, and spare clothes hang on nails inside the bed-places and in the corners. Aft amidships, in a slip of leather nailed to the wall, hangs a bottle of brandy, the sole stimulant we indulge in; and side by side with the more generous fluid is a bottle of chloride of lime, with the cork out, for the purpose of mollifying, in some measure, the awful effluvium caused by the commingling of putrid walrus oil and bilge-water. Vain hope! Add to these little *agrémens* the fact that the thermometer averages 40° in the cabin, and I think it will be generally conceded that we are paying pretty dear for the pleasure of hunting walruses in the Arctic seas. I must not omit to mention that the cabin has *two* redeeming points, viz., there are no vermin, and the wood of which the beams and boarding is composed is of a very light and soft description, eminently adapted for "whittling" and engraving, and in these intellectual and scientific occupations we find a great resource. As for reading, it is next to impossible, for I defy any body to read long sitting on a locker nine inches broad; also, the bunks are too dark, and if we try to read in them we generally go to sleep.

15*th*. Wind round to the southwest, and mild. Summoned on deck at 5 A.M., a large herd of walruses being reported from the mast-head. They were a long distance off, and were not visible from the deck; but, as it was dead calm, Isaac said we had better go up to them in the boats for fear of fog coming on again, or some other boats being before us; so we had our breakfast first, and then started with both boats full-manned. We had a pleasant row of four or five miles over calm water quite free of ice, and were cheered for the latter half of the distance by the sonorous bellowing and trumpeting of a vast number of walruses. We soon came in sight of a long line of low flat icebergs crowded with sea-horses. There were at least ten of these bergs so packed with the walruses that in some places they lay two deep on the ice. There can not have been less than 300 in sight at once; but they were very shy and restless, and, although we tried every troop in succession as carefully as possible, we did not succeed in getting within harpooning distance of a single walrus. Many of them were asleep; but there were always some moving about who gave the alarm to their sleeping comrades by flapping them with their fore feet, and one troop after another managed to scuffle into the sea always just a second or so in time to avoid the deadly harpoon. When there are so many together there is always a pretty fair chance of securing some by "jaging" them in the water—that is to say, by perseveringly rowing after them as hard as possible, and keeping on in the same direction they appear to take when they dive; if there are calves in the herd they can not go much faster than the boat, if so fast; also the calves must come up to breathe much more frequently than the old ones, and the whole herd generally accommodate their pace to that of the old cows with young ones. In all my sporting experience I never saw any thing to equal the wild excitement of these hunts. Five pair of oars, pulled with utmost strength, make the boat seem to fly through the water, while, perhaps, a hundred walruses roaring, bellowing, blowing, snorting, and splashing, make an acre of the sea all in a foam before and around her. The harpooner stands with one foot on the thwart and the other on the front locker, with the line coiled in his right hand, and the long weapon in both hands ready balanced for a dart, while he shouts to the crew which direction to take, as he frequently, from standing upright in the boat, can see the walruses under water.

The herd generally keep close together, and the simultaneousness with which they dive and reappear again is remarkable: one moment you see a hundred grisly heads and long gleaming white tusks above the waves; they give one spout from their blow-holes, take one breath of fresh air, and the next moment you see a hundred brown hemispherical backs, the next a hundred pair of hind flippers flourishing, and then they are all down. On, on, goes the boat as hard as ever we can pull the oars; up come the sea-horses again, pretty close this time, and before they can draw breath the boat rushes into the midst of them: *whish!* goes the harpoon: *birr!* goes the line over the gunwale: and a luckless junger on whom Christian has kept his eye is "fast:" his bereaved mother charges the boat instantly with flashing eyes and snorting with rage; she quickly receives a harpoon in the back and a bullet in the brains, and she hangs lifeless on the line: now the junger begins to utter his plaintive grunting bark, and fifty furious walruses are close round the boat in a few seconds, rearing up breast high in the water, and snorting and blowing as if they would tear us all to pieces. Two of these auxiliaries are speedily harpooned in their turn, and the rest hang back a little, when, as bad luck would have it, the junger gave up the ghost, owing to the severity of his harpooning, and the others, no longer attracted by his cries, retire to a more prudent distance. But for the "untoward" and premature decease of the junger, the men tell me we should have had more walruses on our hands than we could manage. We now devote our attention to "polishing off" the two live walruses—well-sized young bulls—who are still towing the heavy boat, with their two dead comrades attached, as if she was behind a steam-tug, and struggling madly to drag us under the icebergs: a vigorous application of the lances soon settles the business, and we now, with some difficulty, tow our four dead victims to the nearest flat iceberg and fix the ice-anchor, by which, with the powerful aid of block and tackle, we haul them one by one on the ice and divest them of their spoils. Meantime Lord David's boat is carried past us at eight miles an hour in full tow of two enormous bulls, with his lordship sitting in the stern like Neptune in his car, but holding in his hand, instead of the trident of the marine god, a much more effective weapon in the shape of a four-barreled rifled.

While we were engaged in cutting up these walruses, there were at least fifty more surrounding the iceberg, snorting and bellowing, and rearing up in the water as if smelling the blood of their slaughtered friends, and curious to see what we were doing to them now. They were so close that I might have shot a dozen of them; but, as they would have been sure to sink before the boat could get to them, I was not so cruel as wantonly to take their lives. When the walruses were all skinned, we followed the herd again with success; and when we left off, in consequence of dense fog suddenly coming on, we had secured nine altogether—a very fair morning's bag, we thought.

The sloop by this time had got a breeze, and sailed up within fifty yards of us, which saved us a long row with our fatigued crews and heavy-laden boats. During this morning's proceedings I realized the immense advantage of striking a junger first, when practicable. This curious clannish practice of coming to assist a calf in distress arises from their being in the habit of combining to resist the attacks of the Polar bear, which is said often to succeed in killing the walrus. If, however, Bruin, pressed by hunger and a tempting opportunity, is so ill advised as to snap a calf, the whole herd come upon him, drag him under water, and tear him to pieces with their long sharp tusks. I am told this has been seen to occur, and I quite believe it.

The walrus is an inoffensive beast if let alone, but hunting them is far from being child's play, as the following sad story will show:

About ten days after the exciting *chasse* which I have just described, the skyppar of a small schooner which was in sight came on board to ask us for the loan of a gun, as he had broken all his, and he told us that a boat belonging to a sloop from Tromsöe had been upset, two or three days before, in our immediate vicinity, and one of the crew killed by a walrus. It seemed that the walrus, a large old bull, charged the boat, and the harpooner, as usual, received him with his lance full in the chest; but the shaft of the lance broke all to shivers, and the walrus, getting inside of it, threw himself on the gunwale of the boat and overset it in an instant. While the men were floundering in the water among their oars and tackle, the infuriated animal rushed in among them, and, selecting the unlucky harpooner, who, I fancy, had fallen next him, he tore him nearly into two halves with his tusks. The rest of the men saved themselves by clambering on to the ice until the other boat came to their assistance.

Upon another occasion I made the acquaintance of the skyppar of a sloop who had been seized by a bereaved cow walrus, and by her dragged twice to the bottom of the sea, but without receiving any injury beyond being nearly drowned, and having a deep scar plowed in each side of his forehead by the tusks of the animal, which he thought did not wish to hurt him, but mistook him for her calf as he floundered in the water.

Owing to the great coolness and expertness of the men following this pursuit, such mishaps are not of very frequent occurrence, but still a season seldom passes without two or three lives being lost one way or another.

16*th.* Mem. "Johann," alias "Jack," to be second harpooner on trial, *vice* Solomon, superseded for incapacity. The latter bears his degradation with philosophy and equanimity worthy of his great namesake, and descends to the much less honorable position of line-holder; probably he is somewhat consoled for his loss of position by knowing that it will not affect his emoluments, having signed articles as harpooner at 20 dollars per mensem. To be a good harpooner requires great courage, activity, and presence of mind; and it is a common remark that "not one man in a hundred is capable of ever becoming a good one." Jack has been six voyages to Spitzbergen, but has never acted as harpooner before; but, being a cool, active, and energetic fellow, I think there is *the making* of one in him. Solomon never will be one as long as he lives.

Beautiful bright morning with west wind. We have beat back to the Thousand Islands during the night, as our people suppose that the great herds of walruses we saw have gone there. Ice very much dispersed since we were here before.

Dined upon stewed walrus veal—very good meat, and without the disagreeable fishy flavor of seal, but slightly insipid.

Saw no game all day, but one walrus in the water. Calm in the evening.

CHAPTER VI.

Sabbath Observance.—Rewarded for ditto.—Our first Bear seen.—Kill him.—Lose the Sloop.—Quantities of Eggs.—Drift-wood.—Comes from Siberia.—Can not be *in situ.*—Geology of Thousand Islands.—Red Snow.—Caused by Mute of Alca Alle.—Bear Battue, and its Consequences.—Deplorable Effects of smelling Brandy.

SUNDAY the 17th was calm, with heavy banks of fog hanging about. We got an occasional glimpse of the precipitous rocky promontory of Black Point, distant four or five miles. Did not leave the ship, but read Morning Service in the cabin. We never hunt on Sundays, although sometimes the appearance of a fat seal or a troop of walruses floating past is eminently tantalizing, and severely tries our respect for the fourth commandment. I am sorry to state that the greater part of the sealing vessels make little or no distinction between the seventh day and the rest of the week, although some of them compromise with their consciences by refraining from *searching* for animals with the boats, merely attacking those which come within sight of the vessel. I must leave to theologians to decide how far these men are justified by the peculiar nature of their occupation in this entire or partial desecration of the Sabbath; but of one thing I am certain, and that is, that they are no gainers by it in the long run; for, whether it was attributable to our energies, mental and bodily, being recruited by a day of rest, or to the fact of the animals, the objects of pursuit, having time to settle during twenty-four hours' respite from bullets and harpoons, somehow Monday always was with us the most successful day of the week.

Verily a day of rest once a week is of essential importance to man and beast, even if on no other grounds than those of physical requirements.

We always considered Sunday to terminate punctually at midnight; in these regions it is just as light in July at midnight as midday, and it was a singular circumstance (might I not venture, without being deemed presumptuous, to suggest that this might be *more* than merely accidental?) that we saw our first bear a few minutes after this Sunday had expired.

We were smoking our pipes on deck at midnight, and looking at a low black rocky island, distant three or three and a half miles, when Christian said, "There might be a bear on that island;" he took up his telescope in an uninterested sort of way, and, looking for a little at the island, exclaimed, "There *is* a bear on it!" We instantly directed our telescopes also upon the island, but could see nothing. Christian, however, stoutly maintained that he had seen a bear, and that the reason we could not make him out was that he was now walking across one of several large patches of snow on the island; after waiting a little we did perceive a minute white speck moving on the black part of the island; it was undoubtedly "Gamle Eric"* himself, and we lost no time in preparing for an immediate onslaught upon him. Visions of white rugs trimmed with nicked red cloth took possession of our brains, to the temporary exclusion of pairs of walrus tusks of fabulous length and thickness. We started for the island in one boat, but shortly after we left the sloop Isaac sent the other boat after us, in order to take the opportunity of getting some dry drift-wood for fuel. We carefully took the bearings of the island by compass, and rowed hard, as fog appeared likely to come on again. After about an hour's rowing we got pretty close to the island, and observed our "friend in white" quietly pottering about, evidently in search of something—"gathering eggs," Christian explained to us. Multitudes of gulls, fulmars, eider-ducks, and "alcas" hovered about the island, screaming and chattering, and evidently in a state of great perturbation at Bruin's oological researches. We got a small cliff between us and the bear without his perceiving us, and jumped ashore with our ri-

* The people in most parts of Norway have a singular prejudice against alluding to a bear by his name "Biorn;" but they generally prefer mentioning him by some *sobriquet*, as "old Eric;" or in some roundabout way, as "the party in the brown jacket," "the old gentleman in the fur cloak," etc.

fles, in expectation of getting a shot at him from the rocks; but, on gaining the top of the cliff, to our great dismay we saw the bear a good hundred yards at sea, and making great play for a neighboring island about half a mile distant. He had evidently winded us, or heard us trampling on the hard snow: he was about 200 yards from us; but we both sat down on the snow, and both fired a shot at his head as he swam; the bullets ricochetted on the water close past his ears, and feeling that we *must* get to closer quarters, we ran for the boat, jumped in, and pursued him with the oars. We overhauled him much sooner than I expected, and on getting within about forty yards we both fired again, and one bullet going through his jaw, and the other through his brains, poor Bruin floated dead upon the water. We put the noose of a sea-horse line round his neck, and towed him ashore to divest him of the "white rug." While so satisfactorily engaged on the rocks, two bull walruses hove in sight, floating rapidly by, asleep, on a cake of ice. Lord David went after them in one boat, while I walked up to reconnoitre the island, thinking there might perhaps be another bear about the rocks: there was none; but I saw, to my great uneasiness, that a dense fog had come on, and the sloop was nowhere visible: the current was carrying the ice past the island at the rate of five miles an hour from northeast to southwest, so that *looking* for the sloop was perfectly hopeless, and it appeared as if we should have to bivouac for a day or two on the island. The fat grease of *Ursus maritimus* had not looked particularly appetizing, so I began to inspect the culinary resources of our insular prison: the island actually swarmed with birds, and there were thousands of eggs of the eider-duck, the fulmar, several kinds of gulls, and the little awk (*Alca alle*), particularly the latter. Bruin's ravages were quite perceptible, as freshly-broken shells and split eggs were strewed about in numbers, but, unfortunately, every one which I opened contained a well-developed and odoriferous chick, and, although this may have suited the palate of *U. Maritimus*, we were not quite so hungry as *that* yet. Lord David came ashore, having been unsuccessful with the walruses, and we began to prepare for passing some time on the island: first we dragged the two boats into a sheltered little creek, and anchored them securely to the rocks; then we killed a lot of eider-ducks and fulmars by knocking them off their nests with sticks and stones, which they were actually tame and foolish enough to allow.

We next gathered a quantity of dry drift-wood, which is strewed in prodigious quantities on all the coasts and outlying islands of Spitzbergen. While gathering wood, I found a very good walrus harpoon lying among the sand near some old bones of sea-horses. It had evidently been deeply implanted in some poor walrus who had come here to die of his wound. It was somewhat lighter than those we had in use, so we ground it sharp, and afterward used it at the capture of many walruses. I found a very large pine-tree (I think *Abies excelsa*) with the roots on, but much water-worn and worm-eaten, as if long at sea; this tree, as well as thousands of others I have seen, lay far above high-water mark.

Lord Dufferin, in his clever and delightful "Letters from High Latitudes," states that this drift-wood is "brought to Spitzbergen by the Gulf Stream;" but I think his lordship must have inserted this remark without due consideration; for, although a feeble remnant of the tail of the Gulf Stream undoubtedly prevails over the polar current during the three summer months, so far as to exercise considerable influence on the south and west coasts of Spitzbergen, still it is impossible that it can bring *pine* wood with it, as the *débris* of the pine forests of North America can not come within the influence of the Gulf Stream. There are certainly pine forests on the south of Cuba and in Florida, the refuse of which might possibly, by the course of the currents, be directed toward Spitzbergen; but it is obviously not from these comparatively limited areas that the vast quantity of pine drift-wood found on the shores of Spitzbergen is derived. I once found on the beach, near Hammerfest, a large piece of mahogany much water-washed, and drilled as full of worm-holes as it could be without falling to pieces—in fact, perfectly honeycombed. *This* had unmistakably come from the West Indies by the Gulf Stream; and if all the drift-wood in Spitzbergen consisted of mahogany also, I should imagine no doubt could exist as to its derivation; but consisting, as it does, entirely of pine (with the sole exception of some few pieces of oak, etc., which have formed parts of wrecked vessels), I think it is equally clear that it has come from the continent of Siberia. This is the explanation which all the frequenters of Spitzbergen give of its history, and I think, upon reflection, that it is the most feasible one.

I presume that the spring floods in such mighty rivers as the Obi, the Yenisei, and the Lena, for a great part of their course draining a pine-clad country, must carry down enormous quantities of drift-wood, partly loose and partly imbedded in ice, and that this is carried out to sea until it gets within the influence of the polar current, or of some storm, which drives it on the coasts of Spitzbergen. It has been suggested to me that this wood might possibly be *in situ*, *i. e.*, might have composed part of great forests at one time growing in Spitzbergen itself; but, although I do not at all wish to give any opinion upon the very doubtful and debatable subject of whether or not there once existed a milder climate in the arctic regions, still I think there are strong reasons for believing that this wood is not *in situ*, because,

1. Nineteen twentieths, at least, of the visible wood in Spitzbergen lies actually on the shore, just above the reach of the waves.

2. A great quantity of it is on the Thousand Islands, and other outlying reefs and skerries, which are composed entirely of bare trap rocks without a particle of soil, and which could not, in their present state of barrenness, have borne trees even in a temperate climate.

3. It is all much water-worn, as if from long exposure in the sea and rolling on the beach; also, a great deal of it is worm-eaten, and I do not believe that worms that bore wood exist in Spitzbergen. Even the wood found here and there, far inland, and high above the sea, is water-worn.

4. Entire logs, with the roots on them, are very rare either on the shore or inland.

5. Many of these larger pieces bear marks of the axe of ancient date.*

6. Wherever drift-wood is found inland, or above the level of the sea, it is generally associated with the bones of whales; so that I think all these facts, taken together, make up a pretty conclusive case against the *in situ* suggestion.

This island, as well as all the other off-lying inlets and skerries on the south, southeast, and southwest of Spitzbergen (I do not include Hope Island), is composed of a rough, coarse-grained trap

* This *might* have been done since it came to Spitzbergen, and so I do not lay much stress on this argument.

rock, which in places imperfectly assumes the columnar shape. These columns seem very much shaken, as if ready to fall to pieces; and the tops of the columns, as well as all corners and protuberances, are much worn and rounded, as if they had been *half made into boulders* already. They, no doubt, are so; for thousands of boulders, quite smooth and rounded, and formed of the same rock, half cover the islands. These are mostly of an average size of about a cubic foot, and very seldom exceed two feet and a half in diameter. They are curiously packed and leveled in some places, as if they had been roughly made into a causeway for walking on by human agency. This singular appearance I conceive to have been given to them by enormous icebergs grazing over and resting on the islands ere yet they became dry land, and acting to the boulders like a roller on a gravel-walk. Among these native boulders I was a little surprised to find a few very round and smooth boulders of red granite, of about one cubic foot downward in size, as there is no granite nearer than the inaccessible peaks of the primitive ridges in the centre of Spitzbergen, distant forty or fifty miles. There were also some boulders of a hard reddish stone like porphyry, and some small weather-worn blocks of a very hard white limestone, of a description different from any limestone rock which I have any where seen *in situ* in Spitzbergen. It seems to me that all these interlopers must have traveled either from the northeast part of Spitzbergen, or from some unknown country in that direction, as it is clear that they do not belong to this part of the country, and they are evidently traveled and ice-borne blocks.

I saw for the first time on this island the singular appearance called "red snow," a description of which is familiar to all readers of arctic voyages. With deference to some of these distinguished observers, who appear to me to have gone *out of their way* to look for some abstruse reasons (such as "the growth of minute reddish fungi on the snow," etc.) to account for this appearance, I may state that all the red snow which has come under my observation has been simply caused by the coloring matter contained in the droppings of millions of little awks. These birds feed almost entirely on shrimps, and consequently void a substance bearing a strong resemblance to anchovy sauce. It may be that "minute reddish fungi" afterward grow *on the droppings*, but I totally disbelieve in fungi growing on the snow *per se*.

To return to our position on the island. About eight o'clock in the morning we fancied that we heard several cannon-shots in the offing, and the fog having cleared a little, we determined to make an effort to regain the sloop. We therefore rowed out for about three miles, when, not being able to find her, and being afraid of losing the island ourselves, we rowed back again, and had made a large fire, and were about to breakfast upon bear-steaks and eider-ducks, when the sloop appeared in sight, about three miles off, and in a totally different direction to that in which we thought we had heard the signal-shots.

We got on board before noon on the 18th, and, after a breakfast of hot brandy and water, cold beef and biscuit, we turned in for a few hours' sleep.

Many poor people have been left to perish miserably on these bleak and desert islands by accidents arising from fog, ice, currents, and *brandy*. One notable case of a somewhat ludicrous nature, but which might have ended very tragically, took place five years ago, the scene being an island which I afterward visited, about thirty miles to the south-west of this one. A great many walruses had been killed on this island the previous season, and a small sloop from Hammerfest came to the island for the chance of finding bears feeding on the carcasses. They found a perfect flock of bears—upward of fifty—congregated on the island, holding a sort of carnival on the remains of the walruses. The crew of the vessel consisted, as is usual, of ten men, of whom the skyppar and seven others landed to attack the bears, after having anchored their sloop, securely as they thought, to a large grounded iceberg close to the island, and given the two men left on board strict injunctions to keep a good look-out.

They had a most successful "battue," and killed twenty-two or twenty-three of the bears, the rest making good their escape to sea; but this chase occupied many hours, and meanwhile the two ship-keepers took advantage of the captain's absence to institute a search for a cask of brandy which was kept in his cabin—merely with the harmless intention of smelling it, of course; but from smelling they not unnaturally got to tasting, and from tasting they soon became helplessly drunk. While they were in this happy state of oblivion to bears, icebergs, and things in general, one of the sudden dense fogs of the north came on, the tide rose, the iceberg floated, and in a few minutes it, and the sloop along with it, were out of sight of the island and drifting away in the fog. The hunting party had thought nothing of the fog, as they imagined the iceberg to be "fast;" so, when they had flensed all their bears, they rowed round to where they had left the sloop, and were mightily disconcerted at seeing neither sloop nor iceberg. They shouted, and fired signal-shots, and rowed out to sea, and rowed all around, until they got so bewildered that they lost the island themselves. However, after a great deal of trouble they found the island again, and waited upon it for several days, expecting, of course, that when the weather cleared the sloop would return. The weather cleared, but no sloop appearing, there stared them in the face the alternative of passing a winter of starvation and almost certain death on the island, or of attempting to cross the stormy 480 miles of sea which divided them from Norway in a small open boat.

Like bold fellows, they chose the latter chance for their lives, and abandoning* one of their boats on the island, the whole eight got into the other one, with as much bear-meat as they could stow, and rowed for dear life to the south; four rowed while the other four lay down in the bottom of the boat, and being providentially blessed with fine weather, they actually succeeded in reaching the coast of Fimarken in about eight days' time, but half dead with hunger, thirst, and fatigue, as may be supposed. The two jolly fellows in the sloop kept themselves gloriously drunk, and floated about at the mercy of the winds and the ice for many days; but, instead of going to the bottom as they deserved, they had the good luck to fall in with one of the other sealers, which, observing the helpless condition of the sloop, and imagining her to be abandoned, sent a boat on board to take possession; but, finding the two worthies asleep in close proximity to their beloved cask, they were cruel and hard-hearted enough to throw the latter overboard, and then lent them a mate and two men to assist them to navigate the vessel to Hammerfest, where we may form some idea of the kind of reception they met with from their justly exasperated comrades and the owners of the vessel.

* I saw this boat myself on the island, turned bottom up, with all her oars, lances, harpoons, etc., just as they had been left five years before.

CHAPTER VII.

Northeast Gale.—Bears' Grease.—Errors in the Charts.—Geology.—Limestone.—Coal.—Creation of subalpine Flats.—Deeva Bay.—"Fast" Ice.—Bear's Mode of catching Seals.—Whale's Bones.—Glen-Turritt.—Large Extent of fixed Ice.—Many Seals shot.—Become my own Harpooner.—Glacier with detached *Moraine.*

We now attempted to beat to the N.E. against both wind and current, with the intention of resuming our cruising ground near Ryk Yse Islands; but in the afternoon the wind increased a good deal, and the barometer gave indications of an approaching gale, so our people advised that we should remain among the islands, as they said the gale of N.E. wind, which was evidently coming on, would bring down plenty of ice to where we were. We accordingly changed our course, and ran before the wind to another group of islands about twenty-five miles distant, where we anchored under the lee of the islands, and rode out the gale in tolerable comfort. It blew very hard during the night.

19*th.* The storm continues with unabated force, and we have some difficulty in keeping the sloop from being dragged from her anchor by the heavy pieces of ice which are driven against her by the wind and current. It is much too stormy for boat work, so we set the hands to cut up the blubber of the bear and the nine walruses last killed. The skin of the polar bear is very thin, and it is consequently very difficult to divide it from the fat without slicing or injuring the skin: the fat or blubber lies in a layer precisely like that of the seal and the walrus; it is about intermediate in quality between the two latter, and is put into the casks among the rest. This bear was neither very large nor very fat, and only yielded about one hundred pounds of blubber; but an old male bear in high condition sometimes affords upward of four times that quantity.

I believe the fat of *Ursus maritimus* is not suitable for the manufacture of "bears' grease;" probably it has a tendency to turn the hair *white.*

A heavy fall of snow commenced in the evening, and continued during the night.

20*th.* Gale a good deal moderated and clear. Got out both boats and coasted about the lee sides of the islands; landed on several, but saw nothing except one or two seals in the water; gathered a lot of excellent drift-wood for fuel. Thirteen years ago four Norwegian sailors had to winter on this island, their vessel having been driven away by a storm and ice; they constructed a hut (the remains of which still exist) of mud, moss, and drift-wood, and three of the four contrived to survive the winter; the fourth died.

This cluster of islands is exactly of the same formation and appearance as the one which I have already described—trap rocks, imperfect columns, thousands of rounded boulders of the same, and a few occasional small ones of granite and limestone; one of the latter containing fossil pectens and other shells.

No ice to speak of has been driven to this direction by the gale; and as plenty of floating ice is indispensable for the success of our operations against both the seal and the walrus, we got the anchor up in the afternoon, and proceeded to beat to the N.E. again in hopes of meeting it, but wind and current being against us, our progress was very slow.

These islands are most absurdly misnamed "The Thousand," for there are not, in reality, nearly one hundred of them; they are also very incorrectly laid down in the charts as being all about equally distant from one another, whereas there are never more than five or six in one group, and each group is generally many miles distant from another.

Hope Island is placed in the charts as lying due south from the middle of the Thousand Islands, but its actual position is about forty-five miles due east from Black Point, or nearly one hundred miles farther to the N.E. than the charts make it. This latter grave error is notorious among the sealers, and I satisfied myself, by actual observation, that the position of the island is as I have stated it.

Black Point and Whalefish Point are the two promontories terminating the chains of mountains which inclose Deeva Bay, and stretch out like a pair of compasses to embrace the archipelago of the Thousand Islands. The seaward sides of both these mountainous promontories are curiously scarped away, so as to form very steep precipitous faces of bare rock; and at places where it has room to lie, there is an extensive *talus* of muddy and shaly detritus brought down from the sides of the mountains by the action of frost and avalanches: these mountains are each about twelve hundred feet in height, and this may be stated as about the average height of the lower ranges on both sides of East Spitzbergen. The granitic peaks of the central range are much higher, but they are every where quite inaccessible, and are only to be seen here and there peeping out from among the glaciers. Black Point is composed of a dark gray or mud-colored limestone and sandstone of a soft and shaly description, which is stratified very numerously or minutely, and with almost exact parallelism to the sea; only in one or two small places did I observe slight bends or deflections from the horizontality of the stratification; in the lower part of the precipice there is, among the sandstone, an irregular-looking band of dark brown or brownish-black coal, but this, for the greater part, is concealed by the talus before mentioned. The limestone contains a great number of fossils, many of which I collected.

Black Point and Whalefish Point are both very

deeply furrowed from top to bottom, and these furrows being generally full of snow, while the dark gray ridges between them are bare, give the mountains a sort of ribbed appearance, which renders them very conspicuous objects, and visible from an immense distance.

All the lower hills of East Spitzbergen are much of the same shape and contour, and they all appear to be composed of the same shaly secondary limestone and sandstone, containing here and there a band of coal; but on the shores of the great bays called Stour Fiord and Deeva Bay, where the sea is not exposed to the violence of the current and gales from the northeast, the detritus brought down from the mountains, instead of being perpetually washed away from the base of the cliffs, is allowed to accumulate; and flowing each year, or each flood, over the top of the layer already deposited, it gradually encroaches on the sea and forms a muddy flat, which slopes at a gradually increasing angle from the almost perpendicular limestone cliffs to a nearly dead level. This plain gets, by slow degrees, covered with mosses, but is for a long time liable to be deluged again with mud and shale from the mountains, until the slopes of the latter get so much reduced by this process that they assume a more permanent shape. These plains are in some places three to four miles broad, and, although their surface may not have undergone any of these natural *top dressings* for ages, they are generally so very soft and slushy that in walking you go up to the knees at every step. The brief Arctic summer is evidently insufficient to dry the ground from the enormous quantity of water with which it is saturated by the winter's snow. The water in these bays is generally very muddy, from being so heavily charged with sediment washed off the hills by the melting snow, and they are unquestionably becoming shallowed very rapidly. This is a process which, no doubt, is taking place more or less all over the world, and by which all subalpine flats and valleys have been formed already; but there is no country which I have ever visited, or of which I have ever read, in which it can be *observed* to be actually happening so conspicuously and so rapidly as in Spitzbergen, and more particularly around the two gulfs of Stour Fiord and Deeva Bay. The actual creation of flats and valleys by the processes of denudation of the mountains and deposition of the sediment is there laid bare to the beholder so plainly that "he who runs may read." If there still exists any one who doubts the power of present causes to remodel the surface of the earth, I should strongly recommend him to take a trip to Deeva Bay, and he may rest assured that he will come back a wiser man.

On the 21st we were becalmed off Black Point, and, leaving the sloop there, we took to the boats and rowed for about seven miles up Deeva Bay, to where two good-sized islands stretch several miles into the bay, the eastern end of one of them being only separated from a projecting point of the main shore by a strait about fifty yards broad. To the north and northeast these islands were connected with the shore by several square miles of "fast"* ice of one winter's growth. Great numbers of seals lay upon this sheet of ice, taking advantage of a beautifully bright sunny day to bask, but we found it next to impossible to shoot them. We tried a great many times, but never could get nearer than about 300 yards. I do not think the seals saw us or smelled us, because we tried going to leeward, and we tried giving them the sun in their eyes, and we walked and crept as quietly as possible. I am convinced that the well-known difficulty of getting within shot of a seal on "fast" ice arises from the sound or vibration made by one's feet being communicated to him along or through the ice. We did succeed in making two or three successful long shots, but, as each individual villain lay within six inches of his hole, they all contrived to roll in before we got up to them.

The white bear, as is well known, subsists principally on seals, and he kills many of them on these sheets of "fast" ice; but how he manages to get within arm's length of them there is beyond what I can understand. When the seals are floating about on loose drift ice, Bruin's little game is obvious enough. He "first finds his seal," by eyes or nose,

* Ice attached to the shore is so called.

in the use of both of which organs *U. maritimus* is unsurpassed by any wild animal whose acquaintance I have ever made, and then slipping into the water half a mile or so to leeward of his prey, he swims slowly and silently toward him, keeping very little of his head above water. On approaching the ice on which the seal is lying, the bear slips along unseen under the edge of it* until he is close under the hapless seal, when one jump up and one blow of his tremendous paw generally settles the business. The seal can not go fast enough to escape by crossing to the other side of the iceberg; if he jumps down when the bear is close to him he does the best he can for his life, for, if he does not jump actually into the arms of his foe and gets into the water, he is very likely to escape, the bear having no chance whatever when the seal is once fairly afloat. It can not be very easy, even for an animal of such prodigious strength as the Polar bear, to keep hold of a six-hundred weight seal during the first contortions of the latter, and a furious struggle must often take place. That the seals often escape from the grasp of the bear is certain, for we ourselves shot at least half a dozen of large seals which were deeply gashed and scored by the claws of bears. It is evidently fear of the bear which makes the seals so uneasy and restless when they

* I have been told the bear will *dive* to avoid being seen by the seal, and, as we once saw a bear dive ourselves, I can quite easily credit the fact.

are on the ice, as very many of these seals in all probability never saw a man or a boat in all their lives.

When there are bears in the neighborhood the seals are always much more difficult of access, and the hunters, consequently, entertain a deep antipathy to "Gamle Eric," and never omit an opportunity of putting a bullet into him, even if in circumstances where they can not get possession or make use of him when dead.

We hunted round all the open sides of these islands in the boats, then landed and walked up on to the highest part of the islands to see if there was any ice farther up the bay: none was visible from the rocks.

On the top of one island I found part of a whale's skeleton at an elevation of forty feet or upward above the sea. The bones were a good deal decayed, and were partly overgrown with moss, as if they had lain there for very many years.

I shot a small seal, which sank in water about fifteen feet deep, but it being quite clear, I managed to fish him up from the bottom by tying the shafts of two harpoons together. Lord David disturbed a bear among the rocks, which took to the water without his seeing it; but the man in charge of the boat saw him and called to his lordship, who then ran back to the boat, pursued the bear, and killed him in the water.

Deeva Bay is marked in the charts as being unexplored at the farther end, and as if it ran a long way up into the country; so, as it seemed quite clear of ice at present, and the sloop was still becalmed, I thought this a favorable opportunity for continuing the exploration of it to the end. I left the sloop at four in the morning on the 22d, and rowed up the west side of the bay.

These lower hills bordering the fiords of Spitzbergen have a very strong resemblance to the long dreary ranges of limestone hills which hem in on both sides the valley of the Nile from Cairo to Syene; and this resemblance exists both in their size, shape, slope, and general aspect (ice and snow aside), as well as in the solitude and almost total absence of life and vegetation which characterizes them.

About half way up this side is a glacier almost extending into the water, and pushing before it a huge moraine of mud and *débris*, the base of which is washed by the sea, and renders the latter quite shallow and muddy for several miles around.

It is wonderful to observe how insignificant even mountains of solid rock are compared to the enormous power of glacial action. They appear to melt and crumble into dust and mud, like mole-hills, in the gigantic grasp of the "ice-rivers."

I once rented the shootings of Glen-Turritt, in Perthshire, and in that valley I well remember some vast accumulations of earth and gravel, the origin of which completely puzzled me at the time; but, after having seen the numerous glaciers of Spitzbergen, I have no longer any doubt or hesitation in believing that the mounds are the lateral and terminal moraines of ancient glaciers, which filled the glen in times when the climate and appearance of Scotland must have been very analogous to that of Spitzbergen at the present day; when perhaps the seal and the walrus sunned themselves (fearless of harpoons and conical bullets) on fields of ice, drifting about among a "wintry archipelago" of barren islands, and hunted their prey on submarine banks, now fertile land, and rented at £5 an acre. The shells, those insignificant but yet most powerful exponents of the past, show that this is more than mere hypothesis, for most of the shells now inhabiting the Arctic seas, although no longer found alive in British waters, are dug up in large quantities in the Pleistocene beds in some parts of Scotland, and particularly in my own immediate neighborhood at Ballinakilly Bay, in the island of Bute.

I kept pondering and reflecting on these subjects as we rowed along the sterile shores of this gloomy fiord. After rowing about twelve miles we came to a slight promontory, and on rounding this we perceived a long low line of flat ice, extending right across the fiord, which was here not more than four miles broad. This was "fast" ice of last winter's growth, and was the outer edge of a sheet which covered the upper end of the fiord for about six miles of its length. This was the first large piece of "fast" ice I had seen, and the day being bright, and the ice perfectly smooth and level, its appearance was most beautiful. It was covered with snow of dazzling whiteness, showing off to great advantage some hundreds of minute black dots, which possessed incomparably greater charms for my bloodthirsty boat's crew than either scenery or geology; for, by the aid of our telescopes, we soon made them out to be seals, and as the men said that they thought this high part of the bay had not been previously hunted this summer, we anticipated a brilliant day's sport.

There were seven or eight huge fellows all lying close to the outer edge of the ice, and we first opened approaches in form against them. They were very shy, and would not allow the boat to come within shot; but no sooner had they dived into the sea than their unfortunate habit of curiosity got the better of them, and every one of them came close around the boat, popping up their heads like "Jacks-in-the-box," and flourishing their heels in the air contemptuously as they dived again. I never enjoyed more exciting sport than I had for a couple of hours or so, for as fast as I could load and fire there was a great round bullet-head standing like a target in the water ready for me, and as the sea was calm nearly every shot was successful. Without the boat going 100 yards from the spot, I shot dead fifteen seals of the very largest size; but, although I took the utmost pains not to fire until the boat's head was directed straight toward the seal and within thirty yards of him, still I had the perverse bad luck to lose twelve out of the fifteen, and generally had the additional vexation of seeing them sinking out of reach of the harpoon just a second of time too late. We managed to get hold of three immense fellows. My harpooner most culpably missed his stroke at another, as the boat shot past him while he lay floating on the surface, and the iron "drew" out of a fifth after he was fairly struck; three of them sank in water so shallow that we easily felt the bottom with the harpoon, but it was so muddy that we groped for them unavailingly for some time.

This was very annoying, and I felt so vexed and disgusted at thus uselessly butchering these poor animals, and strewing the muddy bottom of Deeva Bay with their obese carcasses, that I was on the point of giving it up, when Christian suggested that if I would take in hand to harpoon as well as shoot, and let him add his strength to the rowing power, we might do better, as the boat was so heavy that it took the remaining men three or four vigorous tugs before they got "way" on her. This change was attended with the happiest effects; the additional pair of oars made the boat start much more readily, and I harpooned and secured every seal—four in number—which I shot after we adopted the new arrangement. I found it much easier to use the harpoon than I had expected, and henceforward I always harpooned seals for myself.

SEAL-SHOOTING.

A breeze sprung up about noon, and we got the sail up and sailed along the edge of the fixed ice to the opposite side of the fiord. The edge of this ice was singularly straight and even, as if cut with a line and a saw from one side to the other. On reaching the east side we landed, and boiled some coffee and ate biscuits.

The spot where we landed was on an immense muddy terminal moraine of a great glacier, the top of which was lost in the clouds and distance. While the men were resting, I waded through sticky mud, nearly up to my knees, to the top of the moraine, and looked around with my glass, and while doing so I observed that this glacier had the peculiarity—which I never saw in any other of the Spitzbergen glaciers—of being separated from its terminal moraine by about two miles of water. This water was mostly covered with ice, partly "fast," and partly detached and moving with the tide; but the slope and appearance of the glacier blended so gently and insensibly into the sea-ice that at first I thought it was all glacier down to the moraine, until at last, with my glass, I discovered that some of the loose pieces were in motion, and observed several seals lying on them and diving into the interstices. The moraine was of mud entirely, and was tolerably consolidated at the top, so as to form good walking; it extended along the entire front of the glacier (which was confined by a limestone hill on each side) in two parts, and was of a total length of about three and a half miles, by 200 to 400 yards broad, and 20 to 30 feet high: the entrance between the two portions of the moraine was not more than 300 or 400 yards in width.

How I wished for an hour of Professor James Forbes to elucidate the mystery to me of this glacier being so far distant from the moraine, the existence of which had so evidently been caused by great immediate pressure from the glacier. There appeared not to have been any contact between them for a long period, as mosses and other little Arctic plants were growing on the moraine. I also picked up specimens of several kinds of shells on the moraine.

In cutting up these large seals, I found the stomachs of several of them containing a bushel or so apiece of small fish about five or six inches long, and resembling young cod.

I believe there are no fish of any size in the Spitzbergen seas, for we tried often with hook and line, and never caught a single one.

CHAPTER VIII.

Large Bear shot.—Adventures of an Opera-glass.—Size and Weight of Polar Bear.—Stories of Bears.—She-Bear and Cubs.—Break-up of the Fast Ice.—Kill the old Bear, and catch the Cubs alive.—Shocking case of filial Ingratitude.

In the afternoon we rowed back along the edge of the "fast" ice, in hopes that more seals might have come out of the covered part.

I was sitting in the bow of the boat, and on approaching the west side of the fiord again I saw a dull white object on the shore, and, by applying the glass, I made it out to be a large bear, evidently snuffing his way up the wind to the carcasses of the three seals which I had shot first in the morning, and had left on the ice near the western side of the fiord. The bear, when we first saw him, was about a mile distant, and the carcasses lay about half way between him and the boat. I was somewhat at a loss, at first, how to proceed, because close to the bear there was a large extent of flat mud and "fast" ice, with several wide valleys beyond, and it was clear that, if we attacked him openly in front, he would take to his heels over the flat, and soon run us all to a standstill, as the bear will easily outrun any man. I then thought I would lie down beside the carcasses to wait for his approach, but it had now got so bitterly cold that I was afraid I would be half frozen before he came; so, after a minute's consultation with Christian, we decided on a middle course, which he said he thought would do equally as well as if I lay down on the ice. We rowed as fast as we could toward the carcasses, and pushed the boat into a little creek, which fortunately existed in the edge of the ice exactly eighty yards on our side of the carcasses. The bear was still snuffing about on the land, and had not perceived us yet, and, the boat being quite white like the ice, it was not likely he would do so now if we kept still. I made all the men crouch down in the bottom of the boat, while I alone watched the motions of Bruin by peeping over the gunwale through a large double-barreled opera-glass, which I generally carry in preference to a telescope for sporting purposes, on account of its greater quickness.

Strange sights has that large, old, battered opera-glass seen in its day, for, besides its legitimate occupation of gazing at the beauties in the opera-houses of London, Paris, Florence, Naples, Havana, and New York, it has seen great races at Epsom; great reviews in the Champ de Mars; great bull-fights in the amphitheatre at Seville. It has stalked red-deer on the hills of the Highlands, scaly crocodiles on the sand-banks of the Nile, and read the hieroglyphics on the tops of the awful temples and monuments of Thebes and Karnak. It has peered through the loop-holes of the advanced trenches at the frowning, dust-colored batteries of the Redan and the Malakoff. It has gazed over the splendid cane-fields of the West Indies, from the tops of the forest-clad mountain-peaks of Trinidad and Martinique; over the Falls of Niagara; over the Bay of Naples from the top of Vesuvius; over Cairo from the tops of the pyramids; over the holy city of Jerusalem from the top of Mount Calvary; and now it was occupied in quietly scanning the colossal proportions of a polar bear, amid the icebergs of the frozen north.

The bear walked slowly and deliberately for some 200 or 300 yards on the ice, as if uncertain whether he should go up to the dead seals or not. How earnestly I prayed that he might not have had his dinner! Shortly he appeared to make up his mind that a seal supper would be exactly the thing for him, and, sliding stern foremost into the water, he swam steadily and quietly along, close under the edge of the ice, toward the carcasses.

I perceived half a dozen of live seals capering around the bear in the water, as if they were making fun of their great enemy, or "chaffing" him, now that he was in their peculiar element, like small birds following and teasing a hawk when they are sure he can't catch them.

When the bear came close opposite to the dead seals he peeped cautiously up over the edge of the ice, and then perceiving that they were not live seals, he scrambled out quite coolly, and began to shake the wet from his shaggy coat like a Newfoundland dog; the instant he concluded this operation I fired, and smashed the joint of one of his shoulders. He fell on his face on the ice growling savagely and biting at the wound. According to a preconcerted arrangement, I instantly sprang out on the ice and ran toward the bear, while the boat started to meet him in case he should take to the water. While I was running the bear got to his feet, and at first seemed inclined to fight it out, as he advanced a few steps to meet me, growling most horribly and showing his teeth, but on my approaching a little nearer he seemed to think discretion the better part of valor, for he fairly lost heart and scuffled precipitately into the sea. I then shot him through the brains as he swam away, and the boat coming up immediately, they got a noose round his neck and towed him up to the ice. He was so large and heavy that we had to fix the ice-anchor and drag him up with block and tackle, as if he had been a walrus. This was an enormous old male bear, and measured upward of eight feet in length, almost as much in circumference, and 4½ feet high at the shoulder; his fore paws were 34 inches in circumference, and had very long, sharp, and powerful nails; his hair was beautifully thick, long, and white, and hung several inches over his feet. He was in very high condition, and produced nearly 400 lbs. of fat; his skin weighed upward of

100 lbs., and the entire carcass of the animal can not have been less than 1200 lbs.

When he was skinned his neck and shoulders were like those of a bull, and his whole appearance indicated prodigious strength. The people tell me that an old bear like this will kill the biggest bull-walrus, although nearly three times his own weight, by suddenly springing on him from behind some projecting ice, seizing him by the back of the neck with his teeth, and battering in his skull with repeated blows of his enormous fore paw; and after seeing the size and muscular development of this individual, I can quite easily believe it.

One can form no idea of the enormous size and strength of the polar bear by seeing the feeble representatives of his species in the Zoological Gardens, as the specimens there must have been caught at a very early age, and captivity, as well as the unsuitable warmth of the climate, prevent them from attaining to half their proper size.

I believe *Ursus maritimus*, in a state of nature, to be the largest and strongest carnivorous animal in the world, but, *like all other wild animals* (with the exception of rare occasional cases), he will never face a man if he can help it; and I believe the stories of their extraordinary courage and ferocity, which one reads in the accounts of the early navigators of the Polar seas, to be the grossest exaggerations, if not purely imaginary. Even at the present day, many ridiculous fables respecting them are current; for instance, before I went to Spitzbergen, I recollect an Englishman, who had passed many summers in Norway, and could speak the language thoroughly, telling me gravely the following story. He heard from the people who went to Spitzbergen that the white bear was a most dangerous and ferocious animal, and always charged right at a man whenever he saw him. "Other wild animals," said my informant, "might charge *occasionally*, but the white bear *invariably* did so, and the plan universally adopted for killing him was based upon this well-known habit of the animal, and consisted in having a spear made with a cross-piece about two feet from the point, and, when the bear, according to his usual practice, charged, the operator presented this ingenious implement toward him. The bear then seized it by the cross, and in his efforts to drag it away from the man he pulled the blade right into his own body, and so killed himself!!!" Upon my venturing to express some slight doubts as to whether bears really were so infatuated as to make a regular practice of so obligingly committing suicide after the manner of the ancient Romans, my friend replied, rather indignantly, "Oh, there is no doubt about it, *for I have seen lots of the weapons they use myself!!!*" Of course, I could not civilly express any farther doubt of the entire veracity of the story; but I must confess that my subsequent experience in Spitzbergen has no way tended to confirm my belief in this very remarkable statement.

Scoresby relates an amusing case of a bear climbing into a boat and sitting coolly inside of it, while the crew, whom he had ejected, hung on outside until another boat's crew came up and dispatched him as he sat inoffensively in the stern. This story, I have no doubt, is true enough, but, upon the whole, I must say that I think the Polar bear affords less sport, and may be killed with less danger, than almost any large wild animal with which I am acquainted. He is generally found either in the water or among loose ice, and, as he can not swim nearly so fast as a boat can be rowed, he is completely at your mercy, and you have only to select your own distance and shoot him through the head. Even if attacked on land, I conceive that a cool fellow with a gun runs very little risk, because, although the bear's speed far exceeds that of a man, still he is so heavy in his motions that he ought to be killed or disabled by the first shot at close quarters. They are sometimes killed with the lance in the water; but it is as well to make use of fire-arms, if they are at hand, as I have heard of accidents happening while attacking bears with the spear.

I have read many accounts of the same nature as the above absurdity relating to the awful courage, ferocity, and invulnerability of the grizzly bear of the Rocky Mountains, but, without having seen the latter animal at all, I feel perfectly certain that he is not a bit more courageous, ferocious, or invulnerable than the Polar bear, or than most other large carnivorous wild animals, and not nearly so much so as either the black rhinoceros or the African buffalo.

It was late before I returned to the sloop, which had sailed several miles up the fiord to meet us. Lord David had also just come on board, and, after talking over the day's adventures as usual, we turned in for the night.

23d. We had only been in bed two hours, when the watch on deck aroused us, and said they had seen three bears going along the western shore of the fiord. Tired and sleepy as we were, this report brought us all on deck immediately. The bears by this time, however, had got out of sight to the north, or toward where I had killed the bear yesterday. The watch said they appeared through the glass to be an old bear with two young ones, and, from the direction in which they were proceeding, I imagined they had "winded" my carrion of yesterday, and were scenting their way up to it like the unlucky individual of their race who had fallen a victim to his fondness for seal-meat a few hours before.

A bitterly cold north wind was now blowing, and a very strong tide was running down the fiord, which, by carrying the sloop before it, was the reason of our losing sight of the bears so soon. As we felt sure, however, that they would follow the shore, we had no doubt of falling in with them speedily, and we accordingly manned a boat—only one, on account of the men being fatigued—and pushed off in pursuit.

During the three or four hours since I had left the edge of the "fast" ice it had all become loose, and was floating down the fiord with the tide nearly entire—at least sixteen or twenty square miles of ice in one almost unbroken sheet; but, as the fiord increased in width toward its outer end, there was plenty of room for the boat to pass up between the shore and the sheet of ice. The tide was running down this passage very hard indeed. A narrow strip of "fast" ice still remained attached to the shore all along where the shallowness of the water had prevented it from floating. We had a row of several miles along the shore before we overtook the bears, and at last discovered them seated on this strip of land ice. Lord David then agreed to get out, and, by running, try to cut them off from the hills, while I should continue in the boat, and row as fast as possible up the edge of this ice in case they should take to the sea. We got to within about 500 yards of the bears before they perceived us. The old one stood up on her hind legs like a dancing bear to have a good look at the boat, and a moment's inspection seemed to convince her that it was time to be off. She set off at the top of her speed, with the two cubs at her heels, along the smooth surface of the ice. Lord David, although an excellent runner, could not keep up with them; so he got into the boat again, and we rowed with might and main to keep in sight of the bears, but they got far ahead of us, and, the weather being rather thick, they had got nearly out of sight, and we began to think they would beat us, when, luckily, they got to the end of the strip of smooth "fast" ice, and before them lay a great expanse of soft mud, intersected with numerous little channels of water and with much rough ice left by the tide aground among it. This seemed to embarrass them very much, as the cubs could not jump over the channels, and the old bear appeared to be getting very anxious and uneasy; but she showed great patience and forbearance with her cubs, always waiting, after she had jumped over a channel, until they swam across, and affectionately assisting them to clamber up the steep sides of the icy places; nevertheless, the mixture of sticky mud with rough ice and half-frozen water soon reduced the unhappy "jungers" to a pitiable state of distress, and we heard them growling plaintively, as if they were upbraiding their mother for dragging them through such a disagreeable place.

We had got the boat into a long, narrow channel among the mud, which contained water enough to float her, and we were now rapidly gaining on the bears, when all on a sudden the boat ran hard aground, and not an inch farther would she go. This seemed as if it would turn the fate of the day in favor of the bears, as we did not think it possible to overtake them on foot among the mud; but

SHE-BEAR AND CUBS.

there still remained the chances of a long shot, as the boat had grounded within about two hundred yards from the bears. Lord David fired and struck the old bear in the back, completely paralyzing her; we then scrambled through the icy mud up to where she lay, and dispatched her. The cubs, quite black with mud and shivering with cold, lay upon the body of their mother, growling viciously, and would not allow us to touch them until the men, bringing a couple of the walrus-lines from the boat, threw nooses over their heads and secured them tightly, coupling them together like a brace of dogs. They were about the size of colley-dogs, and no sooner did they feel themselves fast than, quite regardless of our presence, they began a furious combat with one another, and rolled about among the mud, biting, struggling, and roaring, until they were quite exhausted.

I before mentioned a strong instance of maternal affection on the part of a walrus, and this old bear had also sacrificed her life to her cubs, as she could have escaped without difficulty if she had not so magnanimously remained with them; but I am sorry now to have to record the most horrible case of filial ingratitude that ever came under my observation. When we proceeded to open the old bear for the purpose of skinning her, the two young demons of cubs—having now, by a good mutual worrying, settled their difference with one another—began to devour their unfortunate and too-devoted parent, and actually made a hearty meal off her smoking entrails!

When we finished skinning her, the cubs sat down upon the skin, and resolutely refused to leave it; so we dragged the skin, with the cubs sitting on it, like a sledge to the boat, and, after another tussle with them, in the course of which they severely bit and scratched some of the men, we got them tied down under the thwarts of the boat and conveyed them on board the sloop. On deck, there lay the skin of the bear I had shot the day before, and the two cubs, on being hoisted up, seemed at once to recognize in it the jacket of an acquaintance—perhaps their papa's—and settling themselves quietly down upon it, they went to sleep immediately. In the course of the day we got a sort of crib made for them on deck out of some spare spars and pieces of drift-wood, and while they were being thrust into it, they resisted so furiously that one could almost imagine they knew they were bidding adieu forever to the fresh breezes and the icy waters of Spitzbergen.

CHAPTER IX.

The Ice disperses.—Lose a Bear and Cub.—Pot 600 lbs. of Bears'-grease.—Skins.—Slow going.—Seals attracted by Whistling.—Glaciers on the Coast.—Noises from them.—Submarine Bank.—Shooting Walruses.—Walruses fighting.—Walrus Tusks.—Awkward Customer.—Ivory.—Story of Mermaids.—Osteological Peculiarity.—Cook loses his Watch.—Shoot a Bear.—Cold Bath.

WHILE this bear *chasse* was going on, the sloop had been carried several miles down the bay before the immense sheet of ice which I mentioned as having become detached from the land. As soon as this ice got fairly afloat it began to *star* and open in all directions, and it gradually broke into smaller and smaller pieces and dispersed, so that by 12 o'clock there was not one piece as large as an acre remaining visible. It is almost inconceivable how rapidly a mass of loose ice appears or disappears in these seas.

We attempted to follow the main body of the ice in the sloop as long as any quantity of the pieces kept together, in the expectation that the number of seals frequenting it while it was fixed would not forsake it. During the day Kennedy shot a fine bull-walrus and two large seals upon some of the fragments. I lost nearly the whole day following another bear with one cub, which we marked into the cluster of rocky islands on the east side of the bay, but without success. Although I placed a man armed with a lance as a *marker* on the fast ice adhering to the north side of the islands, and caused the boat to row along the open side, while I beat the islands, like a pointer, myself, still we could not discover them, and I got on board the sloop near Black Point at midnight, rather knocked up, and disgusted at my want of success; for, as we had hitherto *bagged every bear* we had seen, we had begun to look upon seeing one as pretty nearly tantamount to killing him. I only brought in one seal, but might have shot four or five, which I did not fire at for fear of disturbing the bears.

Sunday, the 24th, was a fine day, but dead calm, and we were still drifting about close to Black Point. Some ice appears to be coming down from the northeast at last, so that we may hope to fall in with walruses to-morrow.

25*th.* Southeast wind and thick fog in the morning. We saw four old bull-walruses on the ice, but the sloop had run so close to them in the mist that it disturbed them, and they did not wait for a boat to be lowered.

Taking advantage of the fog, all hands are busy flensing and packing blubber. This is a horribly wet, dirty, cold, and greasy operation, and is generally held on the part of the crew as constituting a claim to a bottle of rum. There is only one teetotaler among them, and I think he is about the *hardest* fellow of the lot—Abraham, the steersman of my boat.

The old she-bear is very lean and poor; but the three last killed, including her, yield altogether about 600 lbs. of fat. *Corpo di Bacco!* what a thousand pities it is not worth 3*s.* 6*d.* a pot, as in the Burlington Arcade!

It is impossible to dry skins here, so the bear skins are thickly sprinkled inside with salt and wood ashes, and then rolled up into bundles and tightly corded. The seal and walrus hides are stowed loosely on the top of the casks in the hold.

We attempted to get through the passage between Halmanne (Half-moon) Island and the main land, but finding the passage jammed with ice, we were obliged to lose half the day going round outside the island.

26*th.* Going *on a wind* under favorable circumstances, the "Anna Louisa" seems to gain about half a mile an hour, or twelve miles a day; with an adverse current, or if there is too much or too little wind, she gains nothing, or perhaps goes a little to leeward. The way in which the beastly tub makes leeway is perfectly incredible.

When I went on deck before breakfast there were four very large seals swimming about, not far from the sloop. Lowered a boat and went after them; shot two of them dead, but lost them both by sinking. When a seal is under water near the boat, it is customary to whistle, or make a noise by rapping gently on the gunwale of the boat with a thole-pin, or any other small bit of stick, for the purpose of attracting him to come to the surface. I was skeptical about this at first, but was at last compelled to admit that "there was something in it." Of course, it is not *always* successful; but the practice is so universally followed by the seal-hunters, and so thoroughly believed by them to attract the seals, that, even if I had never seen it succeed myself, I should not consider myself at liberty to doubt it.

We are still only a few miles north of Black Point, and opposite a glacier extending into the sea. Like all the other coast glaciers, with few exceptions, it is only an arm or branch of that vast body of solid ice which occupies all the interior of the country, and which, like an enormous centipede, extends its hundred legs down nearly every valley to the sea on both sides of the islands.

There are three glaciers on this part of the coast between Black Point and Ryk Yse Islands. The two southmost ones are not of any great size or in any way remarkable. They each have a sea front of about three miles, and protrude into the water for one and a half or two miles in regular semicircular arcs.

The third or northmost of these three glaciers is one of the largest and most remarkable in Spitzbergen, or perhaps in all the world. It has a seaward face of thirty or thirty-two English miles, and protrudes in three great sweeping arcs for at least five miles beyond the coast line. It has a precipitous and inaccessible cliff of ice all along its face, varying from twenty to one hundred feet in height; pieces from the size of a church downward are constantly becoming detached from this icy precipice, and tumble into the sea with a terrific roar and splash, and of course render it highly dangerous to go near the base in a boat. The surrounding sea is always filled with these fragments of all sizes and shapes, and many of them I have observed carrying large quantities of clay and stones imbedded in them.

This great glacier is in three divisions. The northern and southern divisions are each quite smooth and glassy, but the piece in the centre is broken up, and rough, and jagged to a degree that is perfectly indescribable; at a little distance it exactly resembles a great forest of pine-trees thickly covered with snow.

This part of the glacier must have undergone some great disturbance, arising either from its sliding over a rocky bed, or from its being forced through a narrow ravine in the underlying hills. Whatever the disturbing cause may be, it is actively at work still, because we frequently saw enormous *slices* of the smooth division split up and *cave in* toward the disrupted part; and there is a constant succession of tremendous booming reports, exactly resembling loud and prolonged thunder, proceeding from these cracks, and from the whole of the rough part of the glacier in general.

I have questioned men who have frequented the Spitzbergen seas for as many as twenty summers, and they all say that this glacier has always presented the same appearance since they first saw it.

Of course, this glacier has no visible terminal moraine above water; but it may possibly have some connection with an extensive submarine bank, which lies opposite the whole length of the front of the glacier, and extends for fifteen or twenty miles to sea. The soundings on this bank may average fifteen fathoms, with a bottom of bluish clay; it is a very favorite resort of the seal and the walrus, particularly the latter, for which I am led to suppose that the bank produces, in unusual numbers, the mollusca on which they feed.

About eight in the evening we came up within two or three miles of a small schooner, and observing one of her boats to be "fast" to a walrus and her signal flag flying to indicate to their shipmates that more boats were wanted, we took the hint (although far from being intended for our benefit), and pushed off immediately in both boats. When we reached the opposition boat we found them still in tow of their walrus, and many scores of others plunging in the water around. They had kept hold of their victim so long in the hope that he would attract some of his friends to come within reach of their harpoons also; but, as none of them appeared to care about sharing his fate, they killed him just as we came up.

We had hitherto lost so many walruses by abstaining from firing and always trying to harpoon them, that of late we had adopted the plan of firing whenever we got a fair chance, and we found that, by using double charges of powder, and by hardening the lead for the bullets by an admixture of zinc, we could penetrate the hard crania of the walruses easily enough when struck in the right place. It was a beautiful sunny night, and we had a most agreeable and exciting *chasse.* The water swarmed with walruses, and in about three hours we had secured eight, besides two which sank. All of these were either shot dead or so stupefied with shots on the head that they allowed the harpooners to strike them. One I killed by firing up his nostrils as he faced the boat, at about eight yards' distance.

This herd were mostly cows and indifferent young bulls, but among them I noticed one enormous old gray bull, who looked as thick as a sugar hogshead, and was by far the largest walrus I had yet seen. This monster came up snorting several times within nine or ten yards while we were fast to two others, but he was too wary to allow himself to be harpooned, and if I had shot him at that time he would certainly have sunk before we could have got hold of him. These old bulls are always very light colored, from being nearly devoid of hair; their skins are rough and rugose, like that of a rhinoceros, and they are generally quite covered with scars and wounds, inflicted by harpoons, lances, and bullets which they have escaped from, as well as by the tusks of one another in fights among themselves. I have frequently observed them fighting with great ferocity on the ice. They use their tusks against one another very much in the manner that game-cocks use their beaks. From the animal's unwieldy appearance and the position of his tusks, one is apt to fancy that the latter can only be used in a stroke *downward;* but, on the contrary, they can turn their necks with great facility and quickness, and can strike either upward, downward, or sideways with equal dexterity. I have little doubt but that in the amatory season these conflicts are often fatal.

Old bulls very frequently have one or both of their tusks broken, which may arise either from fighting or from using them to assist in clambering up the ice and rocks. These broken tusks soon get worn and sharpened to a point again by the action of the sand, as the walrus uses his tusks, like the elephant and the boar, for plowing his food out of the ground, with this difference, that the operations of the sea-elephant—as he ought to be called, instead of the sea-horse—are carried on at the bottom of the sea.

I have frequently opened the stomachs of walruses, and found their food to consist of quantities of sand-worms, starfish, shrimps, and the shells Tridacnæ and Cardia, vulgarly called clams and cockles. I believe they also eat submarine algæ or sea-weeds, and Scoresby mentions having found the remains of young seals in their stomachs; but I imagine the latter case to be an unusual one, as the seal is a much more active animal in the water than the walrus, and I have never met with any one else who had observed it.

The tusks of the walrus are not an extra pair of teeth, but simply an enlargement and modification of the eye-teeth, produced, as I believe, by the necessity the animal has for long tusks, in order to obtain his food in the way he does.

They are very firmly and strongly imbedded, for about six or seven inches of their length, in a mass of very hard and solid bone, forming the front of the animal's head. This bony protuberance is the size of a man's skull, and through it runs the passage by which the animal breathes, the blow-holes lying between the roots of the tusks. The part of the tusks which is imbedded in the head is hollow, but is mostly filled up with a cellular bony substance containing much oil; the remainder of the tusk is hard and solid throughout.

The calf has no tusks the first year, but the second year, when he has attained to about the size of a large seal, he has a pair about as large as the canine teeth of a lion; the third year they are about six inches long.

Tusks vary very much in size and shape, according to the age and sex of the animal. *A good pair* of bull's tusks may be stated as twenty-four inches long, and four pounds apiece in weight; but we obtained several pairs above these dimensions, and in particular one pair, which measured thirty-one inches in length when taken out of the head, and weigh eight pounds each. Such a pair of tusks, however, is extremely rare, and I never, to the best of my belief, saw a pair nearly equal to them among more than one thousand walruses, although we took the utmost pains to secure the best, and always inspected the tusks carefully with the glass before we fired a shot or threw a harpoon.

Cows' tusks will *average* fully as long as bulls', from their being less liable to be broken, but they are seldom *more* than twenty inches long, and three pounds each in weight. They are generally set much closer together than the bull's tusks, sometimes even overlapping one another at the points, as is the case with the stuffed specimen in the British Museum. The tusks of old bulls, on the contrary, generally diverge from one another, being sometimes as much as fifteen inches apart at the points. It is a common belief among the hunters that those walruses which have wide-set tusks are the most savage and dangerous, and more particularly if the tusks diverge from one another *in curves*, as is sometimes, though rarely, the case. I can easily conceive that this opinion is well founded, because it is evident that a walrus with his tusks diverging at the points must be much *handier* in the use of them than if they stick straight down, or curve inward or toward his breast. I remember once going on board another small sloop, and seeing the skull of an old walrus with remarkably wide-set tusks lying on deck: my harpooner remarked to the captain of the sloop, "That must have been a troublesome customer." "I believe you," said the skyppar; "he put his tusks through the boat, and nearly upset us. Look here," he continued, pointing to the bottom of the boat hanging on the davits, "and see what the scoundrel did." A piece had been torn out of one of the planks, and the hole was patched with sheet lead.

Walrus-tusks are composed of very hard, dense, and white ivory. Their small size rendering them inapplicable for many ivory manufactures, they do not command nearly the price of elephant ivory, but they are in high repute for the manufacture of false teeth, and are also made into chessmen, umbrella handles, whistles, and other small articles.

The upper lip of the walrus is thickly set with strong, transparent, bristly hairs, about six inches long, and as thick as a crow-quill; and this terrific mustache, together with his long white tusks, and fierce-looking, blood-shot eyes, gives *Rosmarus trichecus* altogether a most unearthly and demoniacal appearance as he rears his head above the waves.

I think it not unlikely that the old fable of the mermaid may have been originated by their grim resemblance to the head of a human being when in this position.

There is one very striking peculiarity connected with the osteological structure of the walrus, which I do not recollect to have observed a mention of in any of the printed accounts of the animal. I dare not amplify this allusion, but I fancied that I should be the first to direct the attention of scientific men to the circumstance. On mentioning it, however, to my friend Professor M——, I found that he was quite aware of the peculiarity in question, and that it is well known to the students of comparative anatomy.

27*th.* The cook went out this morning to officiate as harpooner *pro tempore*, and while darting the harpoon at a seal which Lord David had wounded, he threw his watch into the sea along with the weapon. The "Doctor" was so thunderstruck by this overwhelming misfortune that he stood on the ice gazing into the depths of the sea as if he expected the watch to float up again. The seal came up again (although the watch did not), and the cook so far recovered his presence of mind as to *spit* him this time, and then, to the great amusement of Lord David and the crew, he began to bewail the loss of his watch, which had been "such a good one, and had cost him no less than six dollars;" nor was he to be comforted until Kennedy consoled him by the promise of another of equal value.

There is plenty of fine ice in sight to-day, but we have unknowingly drifted too far from the coast, where the water is too deep for walruses, as these animals can not descend in more than about twenty-five fathoms, and they prefer fifteen or even ten fathoms. We discovered our mistake by getting a glimpse of the mountains of Hope Island, and immediately stood in to the westward toward the shore of Spitzbergen, now distant about twenty-five miles.

In the afternoon we put off in both boats to hunt among the ice. I had shot two seals, besides another which, although shot dead, rolled off the ice in his dying convulsions and sank, when suddenly we descried a bear standing on an iceberg at some distance off, and, the ice being tolerably open, it soon became obvious that his minutes were numbered, and that we were sure of him. He stood on the iceberg coolly looking at us for some time, and at last he slid deliberately backward into the water, and began swimming away from us as fast as he could. The boat speedily overhauled him, and when we got about fifty yards from him, he turned round and swam straight at the boat. I called to the men to lay on their oars, and I waited until the bear, roaring and showing his teeth, swam up to about ten yards from the boat, when I shot him through the front of the head and killed him.

This was a large male bear, and I was a little surprised at finding him so far from land, although I have read and heard of their being found at much greater distances. Indeed, there are instances on record of bears swimming across and landing on the shores of Finmarken, although I have always imagined that those individuals must have got out of their reckoning, or been drifted across in storms.

I had intended to try to kill this bear with the lance, but he looked so fierce and so formidable as he came at the boat that *I thought better of it*, and stuck to my trusty rifle instead of trying any experiments of that sort.

While flensing the bear, one of my boat's crew was standing incautiously on the brink of the iceberg on which we all were, when suddenly several feet of it gave way underneath him, and he went over head and ears into the water, to the great merriment of his fellows, but very much to his own discomfiture, and I should think *discomfort*, forasmuch as the temperature was just about freezing-point, and we did not reach the vessel for several hours afterward. This is an accident of very frequent occurrence to a novice; an old hand always takes the precaution of smashing down the hollow or undermined edges of the ice with a haak-pick or the butt of a lance before he ventures to stand upon it.

CHAPTER X.

Boat-race.—Visit.—Ingenious Harpoon.—Hippopotamus.—Phoca Vitulina, or Little Seal.—Phoca Hispida, or Jan Mayen Seal.—Dreadful Smell of Cargo.—Ferocity of young Bear.—Drift-ice.—Stones and Clay on Icebergs.—Warm Day.—Beautiful Caverns in the Ice.—Upset of an Iceberg.—Young Ice.—Noises from Glacier.—Crimping a Walrus.—Ivory Gulls.—See a Bear.—Curious Delusion.—Gulf Stream and Arctic Current.—Danger of getting embayed.—Narrow Escape.

28th. Fog in the morning confined us to the sloop during the early part of the day.

When it cleared, a schooner was in sight not far off, and a herd of walruses on the ice about equidistant from the two vessels. We lowered a boat with all dispatch; but the schooner's people, seeing us do so, lowered away also, and we had a rather exciting race up to the walruses. The rival boat, being rather lighter than ours, got a length or two ahead of us, and we lay on our oars, so as not to spoil the chance for them; but the walruses took the alarm, and neither of us got any.

The skyppar of the schooner came on board in the afternoon to try to beg, borrow, or buy a rifle from us, as he had been so unlucky as to break or lose all the four belonging to his vessel. We expressed our regret at being unable to oblige him;

but, as he seemed a very decent fellow, and spoke tolerable English, we invited him below, "liquored him up," and then proceeded to extract all the information and news we could from him. He was very communicative, and gave us, first, the story (to which I have before alluded) of the poor man being killed by the walrus.

Secondly. Three vessels for Hammerfest, and one for Tromsöe, had gone home full, one of them conveying the frost-bitten skyppar and his five companions. All four vessels intended returning immediately, to try to get another cargo if possible, as August, which is usually the best hunting month of the whole summer, is still before us.

Thirdly. All the ice and all the vessels had left Stour Fiord; four were hereabouts, and four more to the north and east of Ryk Yse Islands.

Fourthly. His schooner was provided with whale-lines and tackle, and he described to me a new harpoon which he had on board. I did not see it, but from his description it seemed to be a most ingenious implement, and was invented and constructed by the blacksmith in Hammerfest. It seems the harpoon is intended to be struck into the whale with the barbs only very little exposed; but the slightest pull or strain upon the line explodes some fulminating mercury in the weapon, and this throws out two barbs much larger than can be readily driven into the animal by hand; and it is thus expected that the chance of losing a fish by the harpoon "drawing" would be very much lessened. The skyppar seemed to have a good deal of confidence in it, but he had not as yet had any opportunity of testing it.

Fifthly. He had killed ten walruses last night, and all by "jaging" them in the water, as they have been so much persecuted lately on this part of the coast that they will hardly sit on the ice at all. He strongly condemns, in theory, the practice of shooting at walruses, but admits that he is at a great disadvantage from the want of a gun, as every body else is shooting; and he says that, when one ship shoots, all the others in the vicinity are partially compelled to follow suit, but that many more walruses would be killed *on the whole* if nobody were to fire.

This may be all very true in theory, but practically I find that every body shoots whenever they find that they can not get within harpooning distance, although they all strenuously exhort *us* not to do it, and seem very jealous of our doing so, which I attribute to the fact of our being much more successful with the rifle than any of these regular professionals. This is readily accounted for, as our rifles, charged with five drachms of powder and a bullet hardened by an admixture of tin, generally smash the walruses' skulls to pieces; whereas the rifles these men use, being mostly light, old-fashioned ones, on the polygrooved principle, charged with a spherical bullet of soft lead, propelled by a small charge of indifferent powder, do little or no harm to a walrus, unless they hit him on the back of the head, just as the occiput is exposed at the moment the animal is commencing to dive. I have found many of their bullets imbedded in the heads of walruses, and flattened out like bits of putty, without having even reached the bone.

A walrus swimming in the water is not unlike a hippopotamus;* but he dives in the manner of a whale, turning up first his back, in a sort of fat brown hemisphere, and then giving a final flourish with his hind flippers as he disappears.

It is almost impossible to shoot a walrus (with any gun) in any of those positions, except, as I have stated, at the moment when he is *beginning* to dive, and exposes the back of his head; but when they are alarmed or excited by a boat, they sometimes rear their whole heads and necks above water, and give a fair opportunity for a quick shot.

The great Arctic seal dives in exactly the same manner as the walrus—I mean, by making a semi-revolution, whale-fashion, as he goes down; but, singularly enough, the small seal of Spitzbergen

* The Kaffirs in some parts of tropical South Africa have a mode of hunting the hippopotamus with harpoons, very much in the same way as the walrus-hunting is now conducted; and this practice in Africa is evidently of vast antiquity, as on the walls of the tombs in the bowels of the silent limestone hills of the Thebaid I have seen drawings descriptive of hunting the hippopotamus with harpoon and line, as practiced by the ancient Egyptians thousands of years ago.

(*Phoca vitulina*), called by the hunters the "Stein-Cobbe," from his habit of occasionally lying on the rocks,* dives by suddenly dropping himself under water, his nose being the last part of him which disappears, instead of his tail, as with his great congeners *Phoca barbata* and the walrus.

The small seal has a very fine spotted skin, and is about sixty or seventy pounds in weight; he is much fatter, in proportion to his size, than *Phoca barbata*, and his carcass, in consequence, having less specific gravity in proportion to its bulk, he floats much longer after he is killed in the water, so that they are seldom lost after being shot. I have frequently shot these small seals from the deck of the vessel while under easy sail, and have had time to lower a boat from the davits, row back to the seal, and lift him up by the flipper.

There is also a third variety of seal found in the Spitzbergen seas (*Phoca hispida?*), the springer or Jan Mayen seal, as he is called by the hunters. This is the seal which we read of being killed in the spring months in such prodigious numbers by the whalers among the vast ice-fields around Jan Mayen's Island, far to the west of Spitzbergen.

These seals, although existing in such enormous numbers to the west, are not nearly so numerous in Spitzbergen as the great, or even as the much less abundant little seal. They are gregarious, which

* The great Spitzbergen seal is never known to lie on the rocks or land.

neither of the other varieties are, and generally go in bands of fifty to five hundred together; they are extremely difficult to kill, as during the summer months (at Spitzbergen at any rate) they never go upon the ice. They do not seem to be prompted by the same laudable curiosity as the other seals, and they go at such a rapid pace through the water as to defy pursuit from a boat. When they come up to breathe, these seals do not, like the others, take a deliberate breath and look round about them, but the whole troop merely take a sort of simultaneous flying leap through the air like a shoal of porpoises as they go along, and they reappear again at an incredible distance from their last breathing-place—whence the name of "springers" applied to them by the sealers.

The Jan Mayen seal is 200 to 300 pounds in weight, and is the fattest and most buoyant of all the Arctic *phocæ.*

Lord David shot two of these seals on the 29th; but we generally regard it as a bad omen to see many of them, as whenever they are in numbers the walrus and the large seal seem to disappear.

One of our men says that, some years ago, the ship's company to which he at the time belonged killed 400 of these "springers" in a single afternoon by the simple process of knocking them on the head with the "haak-picks" as they lay on the ice near South Cape.

Crew cutting up blubber, and scraping and cleaning skulls of bears and walruses all the afternoon. The latter process is a decidedly unpopular occupation, which is not to be wondered at, as it is very cold and tedious work, and they are so averse to begin that they generally leave the skulls until they are in a state which certainly can not add to the pleasure of the operator.

Our cargo altogether is beginning to get so exceedingly *high*, that the chloride of lime is quite overpowered or extinguished by the effluvium, and we are compelled to have recourse to the refinement of *burning pastilles* in the cabin before we lie down to sleep. Fancy pastilles in a sealing vessel!

30th. Our young white bears have now become brown, and are in a fair way to become black with dirt, and tar, and grease, so we took them out to-day, and, tying the end of a rope round their middles, we gave them each a swim, or, to speak more correctly, a tow behind the vessel, to clean them; one of them, the female, is quiet and peaceable enough, but the other is the most ferocious and irreclaimable young demon I ever saw in my life. He was so savage and tyrannical toward his sister that we built a sort of partition in their crib, and since that he has devoted his entire energies, with hardly any intermission, by day or by night, to roaring and growling, while he bites and scratches at the rotten drift-wood composing the cage in an equally persevering manner; we found to-day that he had very nearly eaten his way out, so we patched up the breaches with the pieces of a stove not at present in use. Although they get as much seal, and walrus-beef, and blubber as they like, they do not eat very much of it, but drink enormous quantities of water. They are visibly getting larger and fatter.

31*st*, *Sunday*. It having been dead calm during the night, we have made little or no progress. Very little ice to the south and west, and too much to the north and east, where it is also jammed too tightly together for boats readily to penetrate among it. The vast accumulation of drift-ice in the Spitzbergen seas consists partly of flat tabular slabs of all sizes, from that of an *acre* downward, which have composed part of the winter's growth on the shallow bays and gulfs of the coast, and partly of rough irregular masses which have become detached from the ice-cliffs of the glaciers. Some of these latter pieces I have observed to be carrying large stones, which, by the way, I have frequently mistaken for seals, and very many of them are charged with such quantities of dark-colored mud or clay that the sea is in places sometimes discolored for many miles around by their washings.

This was one of the finest and warmest days I ever knew in Spitzbergen. The thermometer was 55° in the cabin, and in the sun it was actually *hot*. The summer's warmth has had a perceptible effect upon the ice, much of which we observe to be undermined and honeycombed, or "rotten," as the sailors call it. It always seems to decay fastest "between wind and water," so that enormous caverns get excavated in the sides of the bergs.

Nothing can exceed the beauty of these crystal vaults, which sometimes appear of a deep ultramarine blue, and at others of an emerald green color; they look as if they were the fitting abodes of mermaids and all sorts of sea-monsters, but practically no animal ever goes into them. The water dashing in and out through these icy caves and tunnels makes a sonorous but rather monotonous and melancholy sound. In moderately calm weather, many of these excavated bergs assume the form of gigantic mushrooms, and all sorts of other fantastic shapes; but directly a breeze of wind comes, they break up into little pieces with great rapidity.

Christian and myself very nearly got a dangerous ducking yesterday from the sudden break-up of a large iceberg on which we were standing to look out with the telescopes. A large piece of it suddenly, and without the least warning, became detached under water, and the berg, in consequence, losing its equilibrium, began to rock so violently that we had some difficulty in scrambling down again to the boat. Immediately after we had got off it, the berg capsized altogether with a tremendous noise and splash, breaking up into half a dozen pieces as it did so.

August 1*st*. Although still bright and warm, I

first observed young ice forming on the surface to-day; it was about the thickness of brown paper, and there was much of it along the front of the great glacier, and wherever the sea was protected by icebergs from the wind.

I rowed for several miles close along the front of the glacier, and killed some seals.

During the whole day there was a continual succession of loud booming reports from the edges of the smooth glaciers falling in toward the disrupted part. These explosions seemed to alarm the seals very much, and caused me to lose several which I had marked.

The sea in-shore swarmed with shrimps, medusæ, and the little black-winged tadpoles before mentioned.

The "flensing" of a seal or walrus is, in one respect, a most horrible sight, for, immediately the skin and blubber is stripped off, the carcass begins to shrink and quiver so violently as even to seem as if it was struggling under the hands and knives of the operators. This shocking appearance is owing to the contraction of the muscles, caused by the sudden cold; the "subject" is, in fact, undergoing the well-known process of *crimping*.

Whenever a life is taken, there is an immediate assemblage of those vultures of the north, the beautiful ivory gulls (*Larus eburneus*, *niveus*, *glacialis*), which seem to be guided to their prey by the same wonderful instinct as the vultures of Africa or the corbeaux of the West Indies. This is the most beautiful of all the gull tribe, being of a dazzling snowy whiteness, all except his feet and eyes, which are black. They are perfectly tame and fearless, and flutter impatiently about, or sit on the surrounding ice, and even on the boat, making a harsh, disagreeable scream until the flensing is concluded, when they make an immediate onslaught on the carcass; but so greedy and rapacious are they, that they always commence by fighting and squabbling among themselves, as if the huge carcass of a seal or a walrus was not sufficient for them.

Lord David saw a large bear to-day, but he got the wind of the boat and escaped over the fast ice to the north. There is a large quantity of this fixed ice immediately to the north of the great glacier, and I fancy it is the edge of the interminable ice-field extending all the way to the pole.

Several square miles of this ice became detached, and gradually broke up into fragments during the night; and on proceeding to hunt next morning, my boat got beset in such quantities of it that we lost great part of the day in extricating her. Upon such occasions we often have to get out, and drag the boat over large pieces of ice which "stop the way;" and as the boats are not only heavy in themselves, but additionally so on account of the number of indispensable articles we are obliged to carry, this becomes very severe work when these "portages" are long or of frequent occurrence.

The greater part of this ice was out of sight before night, owing to the strong current which runs from the northeast on this part of the coast; this current has perceptibly increased in strength since we came to Spitzbergen, and may now be running at three miles an hour.

When sailing at some miles from the land it is very difficult to realize the existence of such a current, for vessel, and boats, and floating ice all go along together, and it is only on approaching any of the large grounded icebergs that one becomes fully alive to it; but then it appears as if the boat and the small ice were stationary, and the grounded berg sailing past them with great velocity—the reverse, of course, being the case.

The Gulf Stream has little or no influence to the north and east of Black Point and the Thousand Islands, as the ice is always traveling to the southwest (except, of course, in case of southerly gales); but directly it is driven to the south or west of that promontory, it comes within the influence of the Gulf Stream, and is rapidly dissolved—that is, during June, July, and August. After the end of August the Arctic current entirely overcomes the remnant of the Gulf Stream, which has been struggling with it so far successfully as to modify its blighting influence on the south and west shores of Spitzbergen during the three preceding months; and the Polar ice, aided by the increasing cold, comes down in such quantities as to defy the efforts of the now vanquished Gulf Stream to dissolve it. It rapidly sweeps round the coast, overlapping first Black Point and the Thousand Islands, then Hvalfiske Point and up Stour Fiord, where it meets with another stream of ice coming in by Thymen's Straits; lastly, enveloping South Cape, it extends up the west coast until it meets, about Prince Charles' Foreland, another vast body of ice, which has traveled round Hakluyt's Headland; and Spitzbergen is enveloped for the winter.

I believe that the sea itself, to the south and west of Spitzbergen, would not freeze over far to the outside of the shallow bays and gulfs, were it not thus crowded and encumbered with heavy drift-ice, continually swept down from the colder regions to the north and east.

Once the Arctic current fairly gains this preponderance over the Gulf Stream, it is quite inconceivable how rapidly the ice sweeps round the coast and fills up all the bays before it. I have been told that a very few days suffice to surround the whole of Spitzbergen with an impenetrable barrier; and I can readily understand that such must be the case, for, in the end of August, we found so strong a current setting round Black Point, that six men pulling their hardest could not move the boat against it; and I am positive that I have seen the current running among the Thousand Islands at the rate of seven or eight miles an hour!

Woe betide the luckless vessel which at this critical period happens to get becalmed far up any of the long bays or fiords; for when they at length make their way to the entrance, they may chance to find all hope of egress barred for nine months to come—a period synonymous with eternity to most of those unfortunates who have thus been entrapped.

On my first visit to Spitzbergen, my yacht had a very narrow escape from being shut into a little bay, near Hvalfiske Point, into which we had entered for the purpose of setting-up the rigging for the voyage home. A sudden calm came on, and the ice was advancing from the east with such fearful rapidity that I began to think we were in for an Arctic winter. No amount of *whistling* would induce a breeze to spring up; so, after waiting to the last moment, I ordered all hands into the boats, and with some difficulty we succeeded in towing her out of danger. I had been averse to adopt this obvious expedient sooner, because we feared that the strength of the current was such that we should not be able to keep the yacht from drifting against a long and formidable reef of rocks which lay *below* the current; but, by the assistance of Providence, we got clear of both ice and rocks, and drifted into open water.

CHAPTER XI.

Dense and sudden Fog.—Our Hours and Habits.—Supplies run short.—Meet the Yacht.—Their bad Success in Sport.—Novel Bullet-mould. — Geological Specimens. — Part company again.—Medical Treatment of sick Men.—Water up.—News.—Old Acquaintance.—Gradual Extinction of the Walrus.—They are receding farther North.—Nova Zembla.—Illness of young Bear.—Attempt to escape.—Aged Bull-Walrus.—His probable Reminiscences.—Coal and Fossils.—Commander Gillies' Land.—Northeast Spitzbergen.—Bear shot from the Deck of the Sloop.

The thickest fog which I ever saw, even in the Spitzbergen seas, came suddenly down upon us from the northeast while we were seven or eight miles absent from the sloop on the 2d.

I had killed one large seal, and was looking forward with pleasure to killing five or six others which we had marked, when the fog came down like a curtain upon us, and, the ice being very intricate, it was hopeless to attempt looking for the seals; so we made the best of our way to the sloop. We had, of course, carefully taken the bearings by compass, and we rowed accordingly for two hours and a quarter. I then thought we must have made the distance, so I fired two shots into the air, and was immediately answered by the people on board the sloop; we had hit her off to within half a mile!

The instinct of these people in finding their way in a fog almost equals that of savages in traversing a pathless forest; but, for all that, the greatest risk which these Arctic hunters run is that of being surprised by fog among the ice when at a distance from their vessel. The most usual expedient, when practicable, is to go ashore and light a fire, and await with what patience one can the abatement of the fog. This, in my case, was out of the question, as the inaccessible ice-cliffs of the great glacier were the only shore within fifteen miles of us, and Ryk Yse Island, which was the nearest land, would have been as difficult to find as the sloop itself.

When I got on board, Lord David's boat was still out, so we fired repeated signals from our little cannon, heavily charged, and with a wad of walrus blubber to increase the report, but they did not rejoin us until after midnight.

They had been close to Ryk Yse Island when the fog came on, and had taken refuge there until it somewhat abated, and allowed them to find their way back.

This fog did not seem to extend much above the masthead, as the bright sun and the blue sky were distinctly visible above the dense vapor which seemed to float on the water; it was also quite warm during its continuance.

We have now got pretty well reconciled to the state of dirt, grease, noise, and irregular hours we live in, always excepting the never-to-be-forgotten stench from the hold. We generally breakfast together at any hour from four to eight in the morning, according to the weather and the distance we contemplate rowing; dine separately whenever we come on board; and sleep whenever there is nothing else to do. Our hours of sleep vary from four to fourteen per diem. We always sleep in our clothes, so as to be ready at a moment's notice if any game is reported in sight. We found this very disagreeable at first, but have now got quite accustomed and even attached to the practice—so much so, indeed, as to feel it rather an irksome duty to change our under-garments on Sundays.

A more serious difficulty is the entire demolition of the consul's bull, the last of which tough but otherwise praiseworthy little animal appeared in the form of a curry to-day. All our other supplies are also running short, and the bowels of all on board are yearning for fat reindeer venison; so I resolved to take advantage of a northwest wind which was blowing to pay a visit to the rendezvous at Hvalfiske Point.

The yacht was not due at the rendezvous before the 6th, but, by good luck, we saw her also making her way there as we were about half way between Black Point and Hvalfiske Point. Upon signaling to her she bore up, and came within hail about one A.M. on the 4th, when I immediately manned a boat and went on board to take possession of as much venison as might happen to be still uneaten.

I was, however, grievously disappointed at finding that they had only shot eight reindeer during the whole four weeks in which they had had nothing else to do, although they had been lying in Bell Sound, which is considered the best place in all Spitzbergen for geese and reindeer. They had also carefully eaten all the *hind quarters* of the deer themselves, and had left nothing but ten lean fore quarters for us! Geese had they none, but they *had* managed to kill some hundreds of eider-ducks; from the fact of there being no drakes among them, I concluded these had been killed on their nests. It was a long time before they had succeeded in killing a deer at all, and said that, but for the eider-fowl and their eggs, of which they had found great numbers, they would have been obliged to go over to Hammerfest for provisions. They admitted that they had found the deer "*very difficult to hit;*" and, as they could make nothing of the breech-loading rifle, they had been obliged to make bullets for the shot-gun, which I had also lent them, by cutting a piece of wood round at the end, and then boring holes in the sand, into which they poured the lead, and then beat these plugs into a spherical shape. The bullets manufactured by this ingenious process must have considerably improved the bore of my gun by the attrition of the sand attached to them. They stoutly maintained having killed several seals, but "they had all sunk." Seal not being very good "grub," I doubted whether much time had been devoted to the *chasse* of that animal.

I was very glad to find that my sailing-master, Mr. Wood, had devoted great attention to making a collection of shells, fossils, gravels, and other geological specimens, a duty which I had devolved upon him when we parted, and for the due performance of which I had given him copious written as well as oral instructions.

I appropriated the ten fore quarters of venison my crew had been kind enough to leave us, likewise all the eider-ducks except twenty, and, instructing Mr. Wood to go up Stour Fiord as far as the valleys where we had found reindeer the previous season, to kill as many as they could, and then meet us at Hvalfiske Point on or before the 21st, we parted company, and bore up once more for the walrus districts to the northeast.

Two of the "hands" in the sloop, one of whom is the redoubted Solomon (harpooner, disrated for incapacity, and since reinstated), have been ailing a good deal for the last week or ten days, and I only to-day discovered that Isaac, the skyppar, who has charge of the medicaments, had, in his ignorance of the Pharmacopœia, been putting the two unfortunate men through a course of *chloride of lime!* A jar of this had been sent from the chemist's, along with the medicines, for the purpose of counteracting the smell of the putrid blubber. It was fortunate the mistake had been no worse, for there also happened to be among the medical stores a jar of *arsenical soap* for preserving skins, and our nautical Æsculapius doubtless looked upon it also as a mild aperient, or some other beneficial drug; probably he was keeping it in reserve, in case a perseverance in the chloride of lime treatment did not ultimately succeed. I at once put a stop to his homicidal proceedings, and administered to the two patients "Duæ pil. cal. et op. haust. cap.," followed, after four hours' interval, by two Seidlitz powders. I could not by any means make out what was the matter with the two men, although I must own I had some slight suspicions of incipient scurvy, and I was not aware whether, in prescribing as above, I might not be acting with as great a violation of professional custom as Isaac with the chloride of lime; but, except the drugs from the Hammerfest apothek, whose Norwegian names and looks quite puzzled me, I had no medicines but the pills and Seidlitz powders, and to them I should unhesitatingly have had recourse if any thing had been the matter with myself.

We saw Solomon sitting on the windlass shortly after having taken his two pills and two powders. His face was a perfect study for an artist, and indicated any thing but confidence in my medical treatment; I am afraid that it even betrayed a slight suspicion that I had poisoned him, in revenge for his losing the big bull-walrus whose escape I have before narrated.

5th. We are still in the same place where we parted from the "Ginevra," as we can make no progress to the northeast with both wind and current against us. This is the more vexatious and tantalizing, as the brief Arctic summer is slipping fast away, and this is such a splendid day that we keep fancying many walruses must be being killed in the direction of the bank and Ryk Yse Island.

We moored to a flat, tabular iceberg, to fill up the water-casks. Even sea-ice, as is well known, makes drinkably fresh water, and most of the flat slabs have a hollow in the surface filled with water from the melted snow, so that we are never at any loss for fresh water.

6th. We met a small schooner, and heard from the master of the great battle of Solferino, and also that Oscar, king of Norway and Sweden, was dead. His demise does not seem to affect very much his loyal subjects in this sloop.

The Norwegians are in general very democratic people, and not fond of kings and nobles; they also very much dislike the Swedes, and most jealously resent any interference or attempt at supremacy on the part of that people.

This skyppar, Daniel Danielson, who gave us the above intelligence, had piloted my yacht from Hammerfest to Tromsöe when I was grouse-shooting among these islands in September, 1858, and I was glad to meet him again, as he is one of the finest fellows I ever saw in my life. "Bold as a lion, and strong as a horse," he is universally admitted to be one of the most skillful, brave, and successful of all the walrus hunters who frequent Spitzbergen, and from my knowledge of the man I fully believe it to be the case.

He had been obliged to go over to Hammerfest to refit some twenty days ago, on account of the leakiness of his vessel; but, even at that early period of the season, he had taken with him a cargo of sixty walruses and a hundred seals, and now he was back again among the ice in hopes of filling his vessel a second time before the autumnal gales set in.

When the walrus trade was first systematically followed from Tromsöe and Hammerfest, much larger vessels were employed, and it was usual for them to get their first cargo about Bear Island early in the season, and two more cargoes at Spitzbergen in the course of the summer. This systematic and wholesale slaughter soon exterminated or drove away the walruses from the banks around Bear Island; but even after that it was a common thing to procure three cargoes in a season at Spitzbergen, and less than two full cargoes was considered very bad luck indeed; now, however, it is a rare thing to get more than one cargo in a season, and many vessels return home after four months' absence only half full.

From all the information which I have been able to collect on the subject, I calculate that about one thousand walruses and twice that number of bearded seals are annually captured in the seas about

Spitzbergen, exclusive of those which sink or may die of their wounds, so that some idea may be formed of the numbers of these curious and useful amphibious monsters still existing in that country; but it is quite clear that they are undergoing a rapid diminution of numbers, and also that they are gradually receding into more and more inaccessible regions farther to the north.

We learn from the voyage of Ohthere, which was performed about a thousand years ago, that the walrus then abounded on the coast of Finmarken itself: they have, however, abandoned that coast for some centuries, although individual stragglers have been occasionally captured there up to within the last thirty years. After their desertion of the Finmarken coast, Bear Island became the principal scene of their destruction; and next the Thousand Islands, Hope Island, and Ryk Yse Island, which in their turn are now very inferior hunting-ground to the banks and skerries lying to the north of Spitzbergen. Fortunately for the persecuted walruses, however, these latter districts are only accessible in open seasons, or perhaps once in every three or four summers, so that they get a little breathing time there to breed and replenish their numbers, or undoubtedly the next twenty or thirty years would witness the total extinction of *Rosmarus trichecus* on the coasts of the islands of northern Europe.

The walrus is also found around the coasts of

Nova Zembla, but not in such numbers as at Spitzbergen; and he undergoes, if possible, more persecution in those islands from some colonies of Russians or Samoïedes, who, I am told, regularly winter in Nova Zembla for the purpose of hunting and fishing.

The 7th being Sunday, we did not leave the sloop.

One of our young bears seems out of sorts, and shows symptoms of rheumatism, being quite stiff and helpless as to his hinder extremities; we therefore gave them the run of the deck for a few hours, while we had their hutch repaired and thoroughly cleaned out. The sick one, after trying to walk about for a little, moaned piteously, and at last sat down in a corner and remained there quietly enough; the other availed himself of his liberty by eating, or trying to eat, every thing he could get hold of, and then turned his attention to exploring the vessel. He looked down the hatchways and climbed on top of them; hunted through all the boats; clambered along the gunwales and out to the end of the bowsprit, looking about him all the time with the most comical air of inquisitiveness. He was evidently searching for a road to the shore, but not finding any, he took advantage of a moment when nobody happened to be looking, and getting over the taffrail into the little boat hung up astern, he slipped into the water and made play for the shore, distant about ten miles. A boat being lowered, he was soon overtaken and recaptured, but not without a most energetic resistance on his part.

On the 8th we came in sight of some streams of drift-ice, and, seeing what appeared to be a seal asleep on one piece, I went off in a boat to kill him. On approaching nearer him, however, we discovered him to be a solitary old bull-walrus. He lay sound asleep on a piece of ice which sloped very much from one side to the other. We were obliged to approach him at the lower side, in order to obtain the advantage of the wind, and on getting to fifteen yards' distance, he heard us, and, lazily awaking, raised his head and prepared to *absquatulate.* He was a moment or so too late, however, for I shot him through the head, and he sunk dead on the ice, and then, in the most graceful and convenient manner possible, he rolled like a great hogshead from the top to the bottom of the inclined plane, and the boat arriving at the foot of the iceberg at the same moment as he did, we easily harpooned and secured him.

This was a case decidedly illustrating the occasional advantage which a good rifle has over the harpoon; for if I had delayed another second in firing, the walrus would have jumped off the high side of the iceberg, which was farthest away from us, and where it would have been impossible to have harpooned him. This walrus was neither very large nor very fat, but he carried a very fine and perfect pair of tusks, and from the worn state of his molar teeth, and his rugose, scarred, and almost hairless hide, he had evidently attained to extreme old age; and I think it not improbable that he may have been a lazy and peaceful denizen of the Spitzbergen ice-floes at the time when the immortal Nelson visited these shores as a midshipman in Lord Mulgrave's expedition in 1773.

We saw nothing else all day but seals in the water. We sent a boat ashore in the afternoon to collect fire-wood, and one of our sailors picked up a good pair of walrus tusks on the beach.

We also gathered some pieces of limestone full of fossils, and some pieces of water-worn native coal or lignite.

A small vessel becalmed near us had, early in the summer, sailed as far to the north as the land marked in the charts as "Commander Gillies' Land," which lies sixty or seventy miles to the northeast of Spitzbergen. I was anxious to ascertain some particulars about this distant country, but I could elicit no information except that "it was a hilly country, very like Spitzbergen, and that there were no sea-horses, or seals, or even reindeer there."

This vessel, however, had a large number of seals and walruses on board, and, although they said they had killed the most of them about Ryk Yse Island, still I think it not improbable that they actually did so at Gillies' Land, but that they wish to keep the fact of its being so good a place in the dark.

There is no doubt that many of the seals and

sea-horses frequenting this part of the Spitzbergen coast come down from the northeast; and I have often suspected that Gillies' Land, or some other unknown country in that direction, must be the grand emporium which supplies them. A great many are known to exist about the northeast corner of Spitzbergen, which, as I mentioned before, is rarely accessible. No vessel has ever succeeded in circumnavigating Spitzbergen, and, although separate voyages have been made which overlap one another in this direction, still, very little indeed is known about those parts of the Spitzbergen archipelago marked in the charts as "Nordost Land" and "New Friesland."

On the 9th and 10th there was a dense fog, with both barometer and thermometer high.

Rather dull work. We have read all our books; we can not see forty yards from the deck; and the smell from the hold is getting almost intolerable. It changes silver to the color of copper, and copper to that of iron, and actually *turns white paint black.*

On the 11th a slight breeze sprung up, and, clearing off the fog, enabled us to ascertain the very unsatisfactory fact that we are exactly in the same place as we were before the fog came on. Some streams of good ice, however, lie in different directions around, but no seals or sea-horses in sight.

The fog returned as bad as ever on the 12th, but the 13th was a trifle clearer, and, being in among the ice, we discovered two big seals in different directions. We took one each, and killed them both.

Lord David had returned on board, and I was also rowing back, when we discovered a bear on a small iceberg close to the sloop. The people on deck also observed him immediately, and called to Kennedy, who was below, but quickly came on deck with his rifle. The bear looked coolly at the sloop for a little before he could make up his mind that it was time to be off. When at last he did so, the sloop quickly sailed up to him, and Lord David shot him from the deck as he swam under the bows.

My boat being still in the water, we took hold of the bear, and dragged him on an iceberg to flense him. While we were doing so, a seal came capering about in the water, popping up his head close to us, and looking at our proceedings exultingly, as if he was thinking with Charles IX. that "the smell of a slaughtered enemy was sweet." I punished him for indulging in such unchristian-like emotions by shooting him through the head.

CHAPTER XII.

Walruses leave the Banks and go upon Land.—Vast Herds ashore.—Frightful Massacre.—Just Retribution.—Cargo of Bones.—Beautiful Day and sudden Change.—Early northern Voyagers.—Scoresby's Opinion.—Open Polar Basin a mere Chimera.—Dr. Kane.—North Pole.—Scheme for reaching the Pole.—Parry's Sledge Expedition, and why it failed.—Alexei Markhoff's Expedition, and his difficult Return.

THE 14th was Sunday, and continued foggy, but looked a little more promising; and accordingly, on the 15th, it had cleared away, and we had a fine day, with northwesterly wind. We were both out in the boats all day, and brought in one walrus and seventeen seals.

During the fog of last week we had been apprehensive that there were few or no walruses remaining in this neighborhood, as we had heard *no bellowing;* and if there had been any walruses around we could not have failed to hear them, as the weather was mild, and there was plenty of good ice. This day's proceedings completely proved that our apprehensions were well founded; for, except the one we killed (and who had been badly wounded by some one else), we did not see a walrus either on ice or in the water.

Several other small vessels which were in sight bore up for the south in the evening, as if they had made the same discovery; and our people say that all the walruses "must have gone on land now," and that the best chance is to look for them among the Thousand Islands; but it seems to us that among so many islands, and so many hundred miles of rugged shores, we stand but a bad chance of finding them with our slow-sailing vessel.

About this time of year the walruses usually congregate together in vast herds, sometimes to the number of several thousands, and all lie down in a mass in some secluded bay or some rocky island, and there they remain, in a semi-torpid sort of state, for weeks together, without moving or feeding. They do not usually do this until near the end of August, by which time most of the vessels have departed full, and of course it is a very great chance whether any of those remaining will find these trysting-places in the few days which remain before the season breaks up; but such chances are what every Spitzbergen walrus-hunter prays for by day and dreams of by night, because they know that if they are fortunate enough to find the walruses under these circumstances, they may be enabled to kill a small fortune's-worth of them in a few hours.

I never saw a walrus on *terra firma* myself, but I know that frequently on these occasions, even of late years, prodigious numbers of them have been slaughtered by the lucky finders.

At the close of my first visit to Spitzbergen, in

the end of August, 1858, I visited a small island, which I think is the southwesternmost of the Thousand Islands, for the purpose of inspecting the scene of the latest important massacre of this sort which had taken place, and the details of which were afterward related to me by one of the perpetrators. They are as follows:

It seems that this island had long been a very celebrated place for walruses going ashore, and great numbers had been killed upon it at different times in by-gone years. In August, 1852, two small sloops sailing in company approached the island, and soon discovered a herd of walruses, numbering, as they calculated, from three to four thousand, reposing upon it. Four boats' crews, or sixteen men, proceeded to the attack with spears.

One great mass of the walruses lay in a small, sandy bay, with rocks inclosing it on each side, and on a little mossy flat above the bay, but to which the bay formed the only convenient access for such unwieldy animals. A great many hundreds lay on other parts of the island at a little distance.

The boats landed a little way off, so as not to frighten them, and the sixteen men, creeping along shore, got between the sea and the bay full of walruses before mentioned, and immediately commenced stabbing the animals next them. The walrus, although so active and fierce in the water, is very unwieldy and helpless on shore, and those in front soon succumbed to the lances of their assailants; the passage to the shore soon got so blocked up with the dead and the dying that the unfortunate wretches behind could not pass over, and were in a manner barricaded by a wall of carcasses. Considering that every thrust of a lance was worth twenty dollars, the scene must have been one of terrific excitement to men who had very few or no dollars at all; and my informant's eyes sparkled as he related it. He said the walruses were then at their mercy, and they slew, and stabbed, and slaughtered, and butchered, and murdered until most of their lances were rendered useless, and themselves were drenched with blood and exhausted with fatigue. They went on board their vessels, ground their lances, and had their dinners, and then returned to their sanguinary work; nor did they cry "Hold, enough!" until they had killed *nine hundred* walruses; and yet so fearless or so lethargic were the animals, that many hundreds more remained sluggishly lying on other parts of the island at no great distance.

Their two small sloops, already partially loaded, could only carry away a small portion of the spoil, but they trusted to being able to return from Hammerfest with other vessels to convey away the remainder. The result, however, was a very striking illustration of the truth of the adage, "*L'homme propose, et Dieu dispose;*" for on their return they were most justly punished for their wasteful and wanton slaughter of these useful animals by finding the island surrounded by many miles of heavy and impenetrable drift-ice, which baffled all their attempts to get at their walruses.

In their hurry they had not even extracted all the tusks, which thenceforth became any body's property; and Daniel Danielsen told me he happened to be one of the first to revisit the island the ensuing season, and that he cut out about a hundred pairs of tusks. The skins and blubber, of course, were quite useless by that time, and thus six or seven hundred walruses were destroyed without benefit to any body.

When I visited this island six years afterward, there still remained abundant testimony to corroborate the entire truth of the story. The smell of the island was perceptible at several miles' distance, and on landing we found the carcasses lying as I have described them, and in one place two and three deep. The skin and flesh of many remained tolerably entire, notwithstanding the ravages of bears, foxes, and gulls. So many walruses have been killed on this island at different times, that a ship might easily load with *bones* there, and it grieved me, as an agriculturist, to see the materials of so much excellent bone-dust lying unappropriated.

I believe the walruses have since discontinued their visits to the island—probably on account of the overpowering smell of the remains of their slaughtered kindred.

The morning of the 16th was beautifully bright and clear, but the game have so completely deserted this part of the coast that we only got two seals and one walrus all day.

Kennedy brought in a load of fire-wood, and some limestone boulders containing fossils from Ryk Yse Island.

Nothing can exceed the sublime grandeur of a really fine day in these regions: the sea as calm and bright as a mirror, and covered with countless floating icebergs of a dazzling whiteness, and of all imaginable sizes and shapes; no sound to be heard but the terrific peals of thunder caused by the cracking of the glaciers, the hoarse bellowing of the walruses, and the screams and croaks of the gulls and divers. All this makes up such a scene, that no man who has once beheld it can ever forget it. Alas! that there should be a reverse to this beautiful medal, but often ten minutes suffice to change the face of every thing entirely: a chilling blast of wind comes from the eternal ice-fields to the northeast; thick fog, and probably snow, follow immediately; the brilliant sugary-looking glaciers are hidden, and nothing remains of the glorious panorama of sea, and ice, and hills, and glaciers, but a dim, and cold, and misty circle of an acre in extent around the boat.

Such a day, with such a termination, was the 16th, and we were late before we could find our way back to the sloop.

17*th.* The other vessels have now all gone southward, and most of them have gone home altogether, so that I believe we are now farther to the north than any human beings in the world, although only in latitude 78°.* There is lots of heavy ice coming down, and we reluctantly make up our minds to fall back to the Thousand Islands.

The extreme north to which the outlying skerries to the north of Spitzbergen reach is about 81°, and very few people have ever succeeded in penetrating to a higher latitude than that, as it is now pretty generally believed that the accounts some of the early Dutch navigators give of having sailed to 83° or 84° are either apocryphal, or founded upon erroneous observations.

Scoresby, who seems to have been one of the most accurate and painstaking observers, and a thoroughly practical as well as scientific seaman, who had spent his life in the Polar seas, admits never having been farther north than 81° 30′; and I believe with him that this is about the closest authenticated approximation which ever has been made, or which ever will be made, toward the pole *by water.*

From much reading on the subject, and much conversation with intelligent practical men, well acquainted with those seas, as well as from my own little opportunities of observation during my two visits to Spitzbergen, I may be permitted to express my thorough conviction that all idea of a great

* We afterward reached 79°, inside of Stour Fiord.

open sea around the pole is entirely chimerical, and that nothing exists within a radius of six hundred miles of the pole but vast masses of eternal and impenetrable ice, unless, indeed, there may happen to be land intervening.

I am aware that the distinguished Dr. Kane held very strongly an opposite opinion; but the arguments in his book do not seem to me to be of the slightest avail against the overwhelming amount of evidence in a contrary direction.

Hopelessly impossible as all attempts to sail to the pole must ever continue to be, I think, if there were sufficient inducements to undertake the attempt, that it is possible enough to do it by land, or, to speak more correctly, by ice.

The distance from the extreme north of Spitzbergen would be 600 miles; and the only way in which I conceive the attempt could be made with any chance of success would be for a well-provided vessel, with sledges and plenty of good dogs to draw them, to go to Spitzbergen in summer, select a sheltered harbor as far to the north as they could get, and pass the remainder of the fine weather in killing a quantity of reindeer and wild-fowl for provisions for themselves, and seals and walruses to keep the dogs fat and in good condition. Good hunters would have little difficulty in laying in *a hundred tons* of deer, seals, and walruses in two months.

It would be necessary, of course, to winter in Spitzbergen, but that would be no worse than wintering in other parts of the Arctic regions, and plenty of hardy volunteers could be got in Tromsöe and Hammerfest to act as hunters and harpooners to the expedition. The dogs would require to be brought from Greenland or Siberia, with men who understood the management of them.

During the early spring the party would have to exercise their teams, and to get them into as thorough a state of condition and discipline as possible, and, if practicable, they should lay out some dépôts of provisions as far as they could on their intended route to the north. If they then were to take advantage of the first available fine weather in March or April to start to the north in well-appointed dog-sledges, I entertain very little doubt they could reach the pole and regain their ship within a month or six weeks from the date of their departure, and *that* without undergoing any hardships or privations exceeding those inevitable to Arctic exploring expeditions.

The fourth expedition of Sir Edward Parry, in 1827, was sent out with a view of trying to reach the pole by sledge-traveling; but, as is well known, it failed, because they did not winter in Spitzbergen, and they were consequently unable to take to their sledge-boats until the 22d of June, a period *at least* two months too late, and when the midsummer's sun had loosened and softened the ice, and rendered it utterly unfit for sledge-traveling. Parry's sledges were, farther, drawn by seamen instead of dogs, and the pace at which men can drag a heavy sledge is so slow that they can not convey a sufficiency of fuel and provisions for a long journey, and Parry's men were consequently upon short allowance from the commencement of their arduous labors.

In spite of these tremendous disadvantages, however, the gallant Parry and his crews persevered for more than a month, and actually attained the latitude of 82° 40′, which decidedly entitles them to the well-earned distinction of being the "Champions of the North." On the 27th of July, however, their solar observations gave them the most disheartening proofs that they were only making the sort of progress that a squirrel makes in a cage, or a horse in one of those ingenious saw-mills used at the railway stations in America; for while, during the last three days, with incredible labor, they had gone about *ten* miles to the front, the Arctic current had driven the ice *fourteen* miles to the rear underneath their feet! At this rate of traveling, it is capable of demonstration that they would have reached the south pole sooner than the north, and Parry was therefore obliged — but one can well understand with what heartfelt reluctance he did so—to give it up.

I believe, however, that that distinguished navigator always maintained, to the last day of his life, that it was perfectly *possible* to make a sledge expedition to the north pole successfully.

In this belief the late Dr. Scoresby also concurred; and certainly no two men can be named who were more entitled to give an opinion on the subject.

It may also be remarked that Arctic sledge-traveling has become very much better understood since the days of Parry; and one has only to read the narratives of Dr. Kane, Sir Leopold M'Clintock, and others, to see what can be performed by zealous and resolute men with well-appointed dog-sledges.

In Muller's "Voyages from Asia to America" there is an account of a sledge-journey which seems to me to go a long way toward establishing the practicability of the thing. In 1715, one Alexei Markhoff was sent by the Russian government to explore the ocean lying to the north of Siberia; and this gallant fellow, with eight others, set off in sledges, drawn by dogs, on March 10th, from the mouth of the River Jana, in latitude 70° 30′. They traveled due north, as fast as the dogs could go, for seven days, by which time they had got to about the 78th degree of latitude (400 miles in seven days). Here their progress was interrupted by the excessive roughness and irregularity of the ice, and they were compelled to retrace their steps. Markhoff seems to have made the dangerous error of miscalculating the quantity of his provisions, or of overestimating the endurance of his dogs; for, on his return journey, he fell short of provisions, and it was only by the desperate expedient of killing some of his dogs to feed the others that he and his companions got back in safety. For this reason, the return journey seems to have occupied a much longer time than the run north, for he only returned to Ustianskoe Simowie, the place from which he had started, on April 3d.

As Alexei Markhoff had thus traveled upward of 400 miles in seven days, and upward of 800 miles in twenty-four days, there can surely be no absolutely insuperable reason why other people, better provided than he was, should not be able to travel 1200 miles in thirty-six days, or even in less time, especially as modern science has done so much in the way of condensing nutritious substances into small bulk, that the difficulties as to provisions, which Markhoff had to contend with, might be greatly lessened in the case of a fresh expedition.

CHAPTER XIII.

Whales' Bones.—Rapid Elevation of the Land.—Early Whale-fishery.—Shallowing of the Sea.—Trench plowed by an Ice-berg.—Last Day at the Sea-horses.—Successful Stalk and double Shot.—Lose two Harpoons.—Very bad Luck.—Difficulty of shooting Walruses.—Gale.—Wrecks in Spitzbergen.—Insurance.—Kill a White Whale.—Description of the same.—Sail to the Rendezvous.

After this long digression about the North Pole, I resume the narrative of our proceedings.

Early in the morning of the 18th we had got back to Black Point, having been turned out of bed at midnight and at 4 A.M. to polish off seals which came in sight.

At eight o'clock we started in both boats, and proceeded, Lord David to Halmanne (or Half-moon) Island, and myself to a cluster of rocky islands lying four or five miles E.S.E. of Black Point. We did not expect to do much good in the way of sport, so we both agreed to bring back boat-loads of fire-wood from our respective islands if we should get nothing better to load them with. I landed upon one of the islands, and ascended to the highest point to look out; there was some ice visible in different directions around, but I could discover nothing alive upon it, so I set the boat's crew to load up with drift-wood, quantities of which, of excellent quality and in every stage of preservation, strewed the shores of this island.

While they were so engaged I walked about and geologized. The island was in every respect similar to those which I have already described; a great deal of drift-wood lay far above high-water mark, and in positions where it could not possibly have been driven by storms in the present relative levels of land and sea.

Numbers of whales' bones also lay upon this island from the sea-level up to the top of the rocks, which may have been thirty-five to forty feet in height. Those bones lying high above the sea-level were invariably much more decayed and moss-grown than those lower down. Some of them were of enormous size. In one slight depression of the island, about ten feet above the sea-level, I counted eleven enormous jaw-bones, all lying irregularly and mixed indiscriminately with many vertebræ, ribs, and pieces of skulls. Of course it will be understood that these bones which I mention in different parts of this narrative were not fossilized. We found them in many parts of Spitzbergen, and at all elevations up to that of two hundred feet above the sea. I brought home many specimens, which are now in the Museum of the Geological Society. Could an approximation to the age of these bones be in any way arrived at, they would give some chronological data for determining the time which the land whereon they were found has been in emerging from the sea and attaining its present level. My own impression, for many reasons, is, that the whole of Spitzbergen has been gradually rising within the last few hundred years, and that this upheaval is still continuing.

It is perhaps impossible to judge of the length of time which such enormous bones may endure in a climate like this, where they are bound up in ice for eight or nine months out of the twelve; but allowing, at a guess, four hundred years for bones lying at an elevation of forty feet, which is about the highest at which I have found entire skeletons, and adding twelve feet of water for the whale to have floated in when he died there, we shall arrive at *thirteen feet per century* as the rate of elevation.

From the position of the eleven jaw-bones, etc., which I have just mentioned, and from the fact of so many lying together in a slight hollow, I am inclined to believe that *these* are the remains of whales killed by man, and that they were towed into this hollow (then a shallow bay) for the purpose of being flensed there. We learn from the accounts of the early whale-fishers that their usual practice was to flense their whales in the bays; and, in fact, that the whales were so abundant close to the shore, that the ships did not require to leave their anchorage in the bays at all. It was about the year 1650 that the whale-fishery *in the bays* of Spitzbergen was in its prime. Thus, supposing these whales to have been killed in that bay two hundred years ago, allowing three fathoms (the very minimum) for the ship to have anchored in, and adding the ten feet which the bones are now above the sea-level, we have twenty-eight feet of elevation in two hundred years, or very nearly the same rate as I have arrived at by the other example.

The enormous numbers of whales which, in the seventeenth and early part of the eighteenth centuries, frequented first the bays, next the coasts, and lastly the banks lying outside the coasts of Spitzbergen, have now entirely deserted these waters altogether. Nobody ever thinks of going to the neighborhood of Spitzbergen now to catch whales. During the whole summer we only saw three individuals of the Mysticetus. M'Culloch and other commercial writers attribute this migration of the whales to the persecution they underwent, saying that they were all killed or frightened away; but, although their disappearance is undoubtedly partially attributable to that cause, I believe the principal reason to be that the seas around Spitzbergen have become *too shallow* for them: this is the general belief of the sealers frequenting the coast, only they generally put the cart before the horse by saying that "*the sea is going back.*"

I have heard the same remark made by the sailors and fishermen on the west coast of Norway, where Sir Charles Lyell ("Principles of Geology,"

p. 506) has shown to demonstration that the coast-line is rising at the rate of four feet per century.

On this island I observed a farther most interesting proof of its elevation. This was a sort of trench or furrow, of about one hundred yards long, three or four feet deep, and about four feet broad, which was plowed up among the boulders. It was about twenty feet above the sea-level, and extended from northeast to southwest, being exactly the line in which the current-borne ice travels at the present day, so that I presume there is no doubt it must have been caused by the passage of a heavy iceberg while the island lay under water.

We left the island about one o'clock to inspect some small packs of floating ice, and, most unexpectedly, I had one of the most exciting afternoon's sport I enjoyed the whole season, although it was attended throughout with the most perverse bad luck. As this was the last day on which we saw any walruses at all, I will venture, even at the risk of horrifying the sensitive reader, to give an account of it in detail.

We first found five good bull-walruses on a piece of ice. Four were sound asleep, with their sterns toward us, but the remaining villain seemed to be acting as sentry; however, he permitted us to approach to about thirty yards' distance, when he snorted, and began to kick his sleeping companions to arouse them. I had *covered* the sentinel's head, and had determined that he should pay for his alertness with his life, when suddenly a bull with much better tusks lifted his head above the sentinel's back; so, quickly changing my aim, I shot this other bull through the head, and he tumbled forward on the ice, so dead that he lay with his head doubled under him and the points of his tusks thrust into his stomach; the rest then escaped. We found that the bull I had shot had given up the ghost in that peculiar state described by the historian Gibbon (in a Latin note) as having been the last dying position of the prophet Mohammed. To make room in the boat for his skin and blubber, we threw out a proportionate quantity of the fire-wood.

In about another hour we found a solitary old bull asleep on a very small piece of ice. He lay on his side, with his back to leeward, which is the very best possible position for either shooting or harpooning a walrus. I felt perfectly certain of this one, and I resolved not to fire, but to allow the harpoon to do the business. When we got to ten or twelve yards' distance, however, the brain of the walrus was so beautifully developed that I could not resist the temptation of firing, and I accordingly shot him through the back of the head; but, to my unspeakable vexation and disgust, in the act of dying he gave a convulsive half turn backward, and the edge of the ice giving way underneath him, he sank like a shot, only, as it were, a quarter of a second before the harpoon *swished* into the water after him. This mishap was my own fault, and I bitterly anathematized my own impatient folly in firing when it was not the least necessary.

We next found in succession three large seals, and I killed them all. We secured two, but lost the third from the edge of the ice giving way beneath him in his dying convulsion, precisely in the same way as with the last walrus.

After rowing for an hour or two more, we found two lots of walruses on ice about an English mile apart. One lot consisted of four and the other of five, and all were bulls of the first magnitude. We took the former first, and, by taking advantage of a sort of screen of ice, we got within six yards of the *partie carrée* without their perceiving us. They lay very favorably for us, two being close together to the right, and the other two about five yards to the left. I silently motioned to Christian to take the right-hand ones, and, like lightning, he darted one harpoon and thrust the other. At the sound of the harpoons, my two particular friends to the left raised themselves on the ice to see what was going on, and, the instant they did so, I took them quickly right and left on the sides of their heads, and they tumbled lifeless on the ice, one falling across the body of the other. "Hurrah!" thought I, "here is luck at last; four of the biggest bulls in Spitzbergen all secured at one stalk." Nothing could have been more complete and more beautiful than it looked. My exultation was, however, a little premature, for one of the harpooned walruses was selfish enough to spoil this very pretty thing by breaking loose and escaping. As we afterward found, this had happened through the line having got twisted round the animal's body and cutting itself against the edge of the harpoon. I then finished off the remaining "fast" one by shooting him, in doing which I unfortunately smashed the fore part of his head, and spoiled a very fine pair of long white tusks. After flensing these victims, we required to throw out all the remaining fire-wood to make room for them, and yet the boat was up to the thwarts with skins, and blubber, and heads.

We then turned our attention to the troop of five, which were still in sight about a mile off. This lot lay upon a rather large, sloping iceberg; we had no cover, and we were obliged to approach at the high side of the berg to get the wind, so that when we got to about forty yards the walruses took the alarm and began to move. I again shot a magnificent bull, with fine tusks, through the head, but, unluckily, not quite in the fatal spot; he fell on the ice, but succeeded in regaining his feet, and began to stagger slowly down the slope after the others, who had by this time gained the sea. The rowers ran the boat against the ice, and Christian and myself jumped out and ran down the sloping ice to intercept the walrus; not being able to see his head, I fired an unavailing shot into his shoulder, and Christian, getting to the brink of the ice just as the walrus was staggering in, thrust the harpoon into his posteriors; the line ran to the end, and then, the boat being fast against the ice, it snapped like a thread, and the walrus was lost. This had been an old line, much used, and, before leaving the iceberg where we had killed the last ones, I had pointed out a weak place in it to Christian, and requested him to change it or to splice out the defective part; he had, however, contented himself with tying a big ugly knot across the flaw, and at that knot the line gave way; I therefore blamed the harpooner for the loss of this walrus; but probably, under the circumstances, any line would have given way in like manner.

We then found three large bulls, two of which were asleep, but the third one, acting as look-out, kicked his friends awake on our approaching to forty or fifty yards' distance. I shot the best one on the side of the head with two barrels, but all three got into the water, the wounded one bleeding most profusely. We followed them for six or seven dives, in hopes of securing this one; but, although he was very sick and faint, the others kept close to him, and always gave him timous notice when to dive; at last I shot the two sound ones through the head, one after the other; but there was now a considerable sea running, and the boat was so heavy with skins and blubber that they both sank before we could harpoon them. After his protectors were gone, I made sure of getting the one first wounded, but after getting close to him once or twice more, we lost sight of him among the ice, and saw him no more.

The sloop was now six or seven miles off, and we had a weary row of several hours, against a heavy sea, which nearly swamped the deep-laden boat, and prevented us getting on board until past midnight.

No one who has not tried it will readily believe how extremely difficult it is to shoot an old bull-walrus clean dead. The front or sides of his head may be knocked all to pieces with bullets, and the animal yet have sense and strength sufficient left him to enable him to swim and dive out of reach. If he is lying on his side, with his back turned to his assailant, it is easy enough, as the brain is then quite exposed, and the crown of the head is easily penetrated; but one rarely gets the walrus in that position, and when it so happens, it is generally better policy to harpoon him without shooting.

By firing at an old bull directly facing you, it is almost impossible to kill him; but if *half-front* to you, a shot just above the eye may prove fatal. If sideways, he can only be killed by aiming about six inches behind the eye, and about one fourth of the apparent depth of his head from the top; but the eye, of course, can not be seen unless the animal is very close to you, and the difficulty is enormously increased by the back of the head being so imbedded in fat as to appear as if it were part of the neck.

If you hit him much below a certain part of the head you strike the jaw-joint, which is about the strongest part of the whole cranium. A leaden bullet striking there, or on the front of the head, is flattened like a piece of putty, without doing much injury to the walrus; and we sometimes found that even our hardened bullets, propelled by five drachms of powder, were broken into little pieces against the rocky crania of these animals.

On the 19th we had a storm from the southwest, and lay-to all day; as it increased toward the evening, and the motion aggravated *the smell* from the hold to an intolerable extent, we took shelter to the leeward of Halmanne Island, and came to an anchor there about midnight.

The gale continued on the 20th, so we remained in shelter, and sent both boats ashore for fire-wood and water. The wood we procured on this island was mostly part of the remains of a schooner from Hammerfest, which had been lost in this bay in a gale of wind five years ago; it was her first voyage, and they had neglected to make the cable fast at the inner end, the consequence of which lubberly proceeding naturally was that it all ran out, and the vessel drove ashore and went to pieces.

From what I have heard, I am inclined to suspect that a good many of the shipwrecks which happen in Spitzbergen are caused willfully, in order to defraud the insurance-offices. These vessels are principally insured in Hamburg, and I believe the rate of insurance is as high as seven per cent., although one would think that even that was little enough for the unavoidable risks of such a dangerous voyage, without taking into consideration the impunity with which such nefarious proceedings as I have alluded to may be committed in those distant waters.

The 21st being Sunday, we staid on board, and I wrote up the last few pages of this Journal.

About 3 A.M. on the 22d we were aroused by a report of many white whales being alongside. We got up instantly, and jumped into the boats with our rifles. There was a very dense fog, but the bay seemed to be full of the whales, as we heard them blowing all around the vessel. We pulled off into the fog where the blowing seemed most frequent, and soon found ourselves surrounded by twenty or thirty of these animals, showing up their heads and backs, and spouting. They were of a brilliant, shining, snowy whiteness, and when they were near us we could see them swimming under water. We lay on our oars, and I waited a little for a good chance, until at last I saw a large one under water approaching the boat. Holding my rifle ready at my shoulder, I was quite prepared for him, and the instant he appeared above the surface I shot him through the head, immediately behind the blowholes. He disappeared in a cloud of foam and blood, but, upon rowing quickly to the spot, I was just in time to strike a walrus harpoon into him as he sank about eight feet beneath the surface, and we instantly followed this up with another, for fear it should draw. A vigorous application of the lance, accompanied by a peculiar *pump-handling* motion of the weapon, soon settled the business, and, getting a running noose round his tail, we towed him along to the sloop. Many others now appeared close round the boat, the old ones white and shiny, like immense shapes of blanc-mange, and the young ones of a dusky gray in color. I could easily have shot more; but, being incommoded by the dead one towing astern, we should not have been able to secure them, as this whale sinks when dead.

We hove our victim on deck, with some difficulty, by means of two strong tackles attached to the rigging and one of the boat's davits, and proceeded to examine him. He was fourteen feet long, by about ten feet in circumference, and of a snow-white color all over. His skin was perfectly smooth, and rather shiny. The head was very small and round. He had a row of small teeth in both jaws. No dorsal fin. The eyes and ears were both extremely small. The skin was of a curious, gristly, gelatinous consistency, and cut very readily with a knife; it was about half an inch thick, and firmly attached to the underlying blubber, which was about two and a half inches thick, and *measured* about 500 lbs. when packed in casks. We kept it separate from the seal, bear, and walrus blubber, as it is of much superior quality to any of these, and produces a far finer oil.

This was not a full-sized specimen of *Balæna albicans*, as I believe they sometimes attain to a length of twenty feet, and circumference of twelve; but we were very much pleased at having obtained a specimen, as this was the only one we killed, and the only time we had an opportunity of seeing these animals alive. They are rather rare on this part of the coast, although frequenting the bays on the west coast of Spitzbergen in great numbers during the summer months.

There are said to be great numbers of this whale in the estuaries of the great rivers of Siberia, and the natives there sometimes kill them in large quantities by stretching strong nets across the tideways, and then harpooning or spearing them.

After breakfast the fog cleared away, and the gale being now gone, we left our anchorage at Halmanne Island, and cruised about all day. The ice has all been driven away again to the northeast by the late gale, and we were unwilling to go north again so late in the season, as the chances of bad weather are now considerable. We held a council of war, therefore; and, as it was clear we could do little more with the walruses this season, we determined to seek the "Ginevra" at the rendezvous of the Russian huts, and to devote a few days to reindeer stalking in the valleys up Stour Fiord.

We reached the harbor at Hvalfiske Point about 9 P.M. on the 23d.

CHAPTER XIV.

Smeerenberg, or Blubber Town.—Agrémens of ditto.—Discovery of Spitzbergen. — Barentz. — Whale-fishery. — Attempts to colonize the Country, and to make it a penal Settlement.—They fail.—The West Indies *versus* Spitzbergen. —Russian Robinson Crusoes.—Wintering Establishment. —How conducted.—Awful Mortality.—Final Tragedy.— Death of eighteen Men from Scurvy and Hunger.—Ingenious Counter-irritant. — Russian Bath. — Cricket. — Boats sewed together.—Post-office.—Signs of Deer.—Kill three Geese with Ball.—Find the "Ginevra," and change into her. — Nautical Nimrods. — Amusing Walrus-hunt. — Gun bursts.

I HAVE often been asked "what the inhabitants of Spitzbergen are like," but I need scarcely mention to the intelligent reader that Spitzbergen never has been inhabited, unless we include under that term the flourishing summer settlement of Smeerenberg, or New Amsterdam, near Hakluyt's Headland, which was the rendezvous and boiling establishment of the Dutch whaling-fleet during the palmy days of the Spitzbergen whale-fishery in the seventeenth century.

Smeerenberg (*Anglicè* Blubber Town), indeed, arrived at such a degree of civilization and refinement that "hot rolls" were to be had every morning for breakfast; and, if report speaks true, even the charms of female society were not wanting to "emollify the manners" and lighten the pockets of the successful fishers. But Smeerenberg was only a summer settlement, and was always entirely abandoned at the approach of winter.

Spitzbergen (literally "sharp-topped mountains") was discovered and named in 1596 by the third expedition under William Barentz, a Dutchman, and one of the most distinguished navigators of the age, who was sent by the States-General of Holland to try to discover a northeast passage to China, a chimerical project, which in those days caused the sacrifice of even more lives and treasure than the search after a northwest passage in later times. Barentz himself, and a number of his crew, lost their lives on this expedition; and the remainder only escaped by taking to their boats, after passing a winter of incredible hardships on the coast of Nova Zembla, where they had got beset, and were compelled to abandon their vessel.

In the early part of the seventeenth century Spitzbergen became the seat of the most flourishing whale-fishery that ever existed, as many as between 400 and 500 sail of vessels, principally Dutch and Hamburgers, resorting there in a season. It then became obvious that it would be very advantageous if something in the shape of a permanent settlement or colony could be founded in Spitzbergen; and the merchants engaged in the trade offered rewards to their crews, to induce some of them to make the hazardous experiment of trying whether human life could be supported there during the winter. For a long time this was believed to be impossible; and, as no volunteers could be prevailed upon to risk their lives in the solution of the interesting problem, an English company hit upon the ingenious and economical idea of trying it upon some criminals who were under sentence of death in London. Accordingly, they procured "a grant" of these culprits—probably sheep-stealers, papists, or some such atrocious criminals—and offered them their lives on condition that they would pass, or try to pass, one winter in Spitzbergen. Of course they were glad to purchase their lives on any terms, and at once acceded to the conditions. They were taken out in one of the whalers, and a hut was erected for their winter-quarters; but when the fleet was about to depart, and they saw the awful gloomy hills, already white with the early snows, and felt the howling gales of northeast wind, their hearts utterly failed them, and they entreated the captain who had charge of them to take them back to London and let them be hanged, in pursuance of their original sentence, rather than leave them to perish in such a horrible country! The captain seems to have had more of the "milk of human kindness" in him than his philanthropic employers, for he acceded to their request, and took them back to London. As hanging them would not have been of any pecuniary benefit to the company, they were then good enough to procure a pardon for the men.

This story reminds me of a conversation which I once heard some of my yacht's crew holding together. They were discussing the respective merits of hot and cold countries—the West Indies *versus* Spitzbergen; and one fellow was urging that, although "neither rum nor tobacco grew in Spitzbergen," still, the continual "blow-out" of fat reindeer which it seemed to afford might be considered as a point in its favor. To him the other: "Well, Bob, all I can say is, that I would a deuced sight rather go to the West Indies and be hanged there, than die a natural death in this here —— country!"

Soon after the failure of the criminal plan, the experiment of wintering in Spitzbergen was involuntarily tried by four Russian sailors, whose vessel was lost or driven away by ice while they were ashore on a desolate part of the east division of the island. These poor fellows had nothing but what they stood up in, with one gun and a few charges of ammunition; but they appear to have been men of a very different stamp from the London jail-birds, and they at once set to work to make the best of things. They built a hut, and killed some reindeer with their gun, and then, their ammunition being exhausted, they manufactured bows and arrows, spears and harpoons, of drift-wood. They pointed their weapons with bones and pieces of their now useless gun, and twisted their bowstrings out of reindeers' entrails. They made traps and nets for birds and foxes. With these rude and imperfect weapons they not only provided themselves with food and raiment, but kept off the assaults of the Polar bears. It is almost incredible; but these men not only survived, but preserved good health for six long years. It seems extraordinary that such energetic fellows as they clearly were should not, in all that time, have contrived to travel across the country, or round the shore, to the west coast, where they would have been certain of relief every summer, especially as they were on the most desolate part of the island, and one often inaccessible, and always little frequented by the whalers. In the sixth year of their captivity one of the four died, and the survivors began to lose all hope of deliverance, and to fall into a state of despondence, which would certainly have soon proved fatal to them all had not a vessel at this time fortunately approached the coast and rescued them. During their long banishment these poor Robinson Crusoes had killed such quantities of bears, deer, seals, and foxes, that the proceeds of the skins and blubber made a small fortune for them.

Other parties of winterers were left on these desolate shores, both accidentally and intentionally; and although in some cases they all miserably perished, still the possibility of maintaining life throughout the horrors of a Spitzbergen winter was made manifest, and a company of Russian traders in Archangel organized a regular wintering establishment, for the purpose of hunting the seal and the walrus, the Polar bear and the reindeer. Their men were left there in September or October, and were distributed in small parties of two, three, or four individuals each, in wooden huts, which had been constructed in Archangel, and were erected in different parts of the coasts and islands of Spitzbergen. The men were paid by a share of the proceeds, and were supplied by their employers with provisions, consisting principally of rye meal, salt pork, and tea. They had a sort of head-quarters establishment at Hvalfiske Point, which was under the charge of a superintendent or clerk, who distributed the supplies to the hunters, and collected the skins and blubber from the different outposts; and the company sent over a vessel in the month of May every year to relieve the men and carry the proceeds of their labors to Archangel.

It was probably found to be too severe a strain upon the constitution to pass successive winters in this way, as I believe it was usual for these men only to remain every alternate winter in Spitzbergen. In 1858 I was informed there was still living at Kola, in Lapland, an aged Russian who had actually wintered thirty-five alternate seasons at Spitzbergen. Many of these hardy fellows, however, succumbed to scurvy and the hardships they endured; and many hundreds must have thus miserably perished, as the traveler in these awful solitudes frequently comes across the ruins of a small log hut, with two or three green mounds or cairns of stones in front of it; and it is also common enough to see the skeletons of the hapless Russians bleaching alongside of those of the bears and reindeer they had killed and subsisted on while living. They seem to have killed an immense quantity of animals of different sorts, and the consequent profits must have been large, as, in spite of the number of lives which were lost, the establishment was kept up until about seven or eight years ago, when such a dismal tragedy occurred at Hvalfiske Point that the company was broken up, and I believe no one has ever since wintered in Spitzbergen.

During the summer of the year* in question a prodigious quantity of heavy drift-ice surrounded Hvalfiske Point and all the southern coast of East Spitzbergen. The men belonging to the Russian establishment had all come in from the various outposts, and were assembled at the head-quarters to the number of eighteen, waiting to be relieved by the annual vessel from Archangel. By a concurrence of bad fortune, this vessel was lost on her voyage over, and was never heard of again. The crews of the other vessels in Spitzbergen knew nothing of these men, or, if they did, they naturally supposed that the care of relieving them might safe-

* I forget the precise date, but I think it was either 1850 or 1851.

ly be left to their own vessel, as nothing was yet known of her loss either there or at Archangel. The ice in the summer months prevented any vessel from accidentally approaching Hvalfiske Point, and no one went near it until the end of August, when a party of Norwegians, who had lost their own vessel, traveled along the shore to seek for assistance from the Russian establishment; but, on approaching the huts, they were horror-struck to find its inmates all dead. Fourteen of the unhappy men had recently been buried in shallow graves in front of the huts, two lay dead just outside the threshold, and the remaining two were lying dead inside, one on the floor and the other in bed. The latter was the superintendent, who had been able to read and write, and a journal-book lying beside him contained a record of their sad fate.

It appeared that early in the season scurvy of a malignant character had attacked them; some had died at the out-stations, and the survivors had with difficulty assembled at the head-quarter station, and were in hopes of being speedily relieved by the vessel; but the latter not arriving, their stores got exhausted, and the unusual quantity of ice surrounding the coast prevented them from getting seals or wild-fowl on the sea or the shore. In addition to the scurvy, they then had the horrors of hunger to contend with, and they gradually died one after another, and were buried by their surviving companions, until at last only four remained. Then two more died, and the other two, not having strength to bury them, dragged their bodies outside the hut and left them there. These two then lay down in bed together to await their own fate, and when one of them died, the last man—the writer of the journal—had only sufficient strength remaining to push his dead companion out of the bed on the floor, and had soon afterward expired himself, only a few days before the Norwegian party arrived. The Russians had a large pinnace in the harbor and several small boats on shore, but the ice at first prevented them reaching the open sea, and latterly, when the ice opened out, those who survived so long were much too weak to make any use of the boats. The shipwrecked Norwegians, therefore, took advantage of the pinnace to effect their own escape to Hammerfest, carrying with them the poor superintendent's journal, which the Russian consul at that port transmitted to Archangel.

When I first visited this spot in 1858, I took a photograph of it.

Every thing then remained almost exactly as the unfortunate Russians left it, and some of their weapons, cooking utensils, and ragged fragments of clothes and bedding lay scattered around. A great many skulls and bones of bears, foxes, deer, seals, and walruses also testified to their success as hunters. We likewise found a curious implement, like a miniature wooden rake, the use of which contrivance was a complete enigma to me until our pilot explained that such were commonly used by the Russians when they suffered from entomological annoyances.

The huts were all formed of logs dovetailed into one another at the corners, and were tolerably entire except the roofs, which had been flat and covered with earth, but had now mostly fallen in. The principal one, about twenty-four feet square, had been used both as sitting-room and dormitory; off this was a small wing with a brick fire-place, evidently used as a kitchen. Another hut was the store-house, and a third—of all things in the world—a Russian bath-house of a rude description, in which I suppose they had enjoyed the national luxury of parboiling themselves, and then rolling in the snow at a temperature of $-50°$ or so. The roof of the main hut had fallen in, and a little glacier, about as large as a boat turned bottom up, had formed in the middle of the floor. On a gentle eminence, at a distance of two or three hundred yards from the huts, they had built up a sort of look-out house of loose stones, and here we may conceive they passed alternately many weary hours in watching the ice-laden sea before them.

They may even have been tantalized by seeing the topsails of vessels passing outside of the icy barrier, but far beyond their reach. On a little piece of level ground, not far from the huts, they had kept themselves in exercise by playing at a game resembling cricket, as was evident by the bats and rude wooden balls they had used still lying on the mossy ground. Altogether there was something inexpressibly sad and desolate about the remains of this unfortunate establishment; and by the rude Norwegian sealers the place is regarded with a degree of superstitious awe, which perhaps may be the reason for the huts being in such a good state of preservation. As my English sailors were not afflicted with any similar scruples, and as we were in urgent need of fire-wood, we took the liberty of appropriating some pieces of one of the outhouses, although I would not allow the standing parts of the walls to be pulled down, in case the huts might be called upon to do duty again as winter-quarters for any shipwrecked crew. We also broke up a large boat, which never could have been made seaworthy again, and which, having been thickly smeared with pitch, made excellent fire-wood. This boat, instead of being fastened together with metal nails or rivets, had been *sewed* together with twigs or withes of twisted birch, and was even then surprisingly strong, the birchen withes remaining quite sound and undecayed. This construction of boat is, I believe, commonly used in Siberia and Russian Lapland.

We arrived in the "Anna Louisa" off Hvalfiske Point on the evening of the 23d, and were surprised not to find the yacht in the harbor; so we took a boat, and landed to see if Mr. Wood had left any letters in the post-office to say where he was. On entering the door, I pointed out to Kennedy my name and that of my yacht, which—*more Britannorum*—I had engraved on the lintel in letters three inches long on my visit the previous year. Hung up by a rope-yarn to one of the ceiling-beams we found a letter from Mr. Wood, saying that he had been obliged by the gale of the 19th and 20th to leave that harbor, and take refuge in another a few miles to the north. As the night was fine, Kennedy and myself decided on walking there, and so we sent our boat's crew on board the sloop and set off alone, thinking the distance was only two or three miles, and that we might fall in with some geese on the way. To the north and east was an immense flat, at least five or six miles in breadth, extending from the shore to the hills; it was dead level, and beautifully green, with mosses slightly intersprinkled with grass, and looked as if it ought to be a very good place for deer, but we could see none. This part of the island is very little frequented by deer in the summer months, although they are said to come down here in immense numbers during winter. The plain was strewed with quantities of their cast horns and tufts of winter hair. We saw vast flocks of Brent or Bernacle geese (*Anas Bernicla*) pasturing on the plain, but as these birds in the winter get the benefit of enlarging their minds by a European education, they took quite as good care of themselves as they do when they are "down South." The walking across the flat was awfully bad, as we went nearly up to the knees in the soft, splashy, mossy ground at every step, so we took toward the shore, intending to follow it up until we should find the harbor mentioned by Mr. Wood's letter. The shore was also very bad walking, and after traveling much farther than we had expected, and seeing nothing of the yacht, we began to think there must be some mistake; and not being in good walking condition after our long confinement in the sloop, we began also to get tired, and to think we should have to pass the night on the shore. We determined not to pass it supperless, at all events, if we could help it; so, observing a large flock of geese in a sort of creek on the shore, with a ridge of trap rocks on one side of them, we commenced to stalk them, in hopes of getting near enough to kill one with our rifles. When we got behind the rocks we agreed *sotto voce* that I should fire first; so, peering over the rocks, I saw the geese all busy guzzling among the mud, and, taking a cool aim, I was lucky enough to send rifle-balls through two of them by a right and left shot; they were young birds, and were slow in getting on the wing, which enabled Lord David, by a beautiful shot, to knock over a third as they *squattered* along the surface of the water. (N. B.—Nothing makes a man shoot so well as the fact of his dinner depending on the shot.) We then walked about a mile or so farther, until we found a sheltered corner among the rocks, with lots of drift-wood lying about it; here we agreed to pass the night, and I set about gathering the materials for a fire, and commenced to pluck the geese, while Kennedy walked to the top of a neighboring rocky eminence to take one more look for the yacht. After a while I saw him with my glass beckoning to me; so, concluding that he had discovered her, I took up the geese and joined him, when I also saw the yacht's topmasts, but still a long way off—above a snug little rock-encompassed cove, where she was perfectly sheltered and almost hidden. We got on board about 4 A.M., not sorry to exchange broiled goose and a bed on the rocks for a supper of reindeer cutlets, with hot brandy and water, and comfortable cots.

24*th.* While we were asleep the crew got the anchor up, and sailed down to where we had left the sloop. Our intention being to go in quest of deer up Wybe Jan's Water, where there was not now much chance of ice, we left the slow-sailing sloop in the anchorage at the Russian huts, and took out of her the two servants and a portion of our *kits;* also Christian and Johann, with the two walrus-boats and tackle, in case we should unexpectedly fall in with walruses or seals. We then ran up the fiord before a slashing breeze at ten or eleven knots an hour, a rate of speed which seemed to us little short of miraculous, after the performances of the "Anna Louisa."

The yacht's crew were all in good health and

spirits. They had killed seven fat reindeer and one seal, after an expenditure of between five and six hundred rounds of ammunition. The British sailor is generally a most enthusiastic but lamentably unsuccessful sportsman, and we were exceedingly amused by the way they described their sporting exploits. The mate told me "he never saw hanimals so hard to kill as the reindeer in his life." "Why, sir," said he, "there was one fellow I fired at, and broke his hind leg—broke it right off, sir—and even that didn't kill him; and, Lord bless you, sir, he ran much faster on three legs than I could. Then I shot him through the head, sir, and made his jaw hang down; but even that didn't kill him, till I got up nearer him and gave him a settler."

Another sailor gravely told me that he had fired at a white whale from the beach and wounded him, upon which the infuriated monster ran right ashore in its frantic efforts "*to get at him.*"

Their description of a walrus-hunt, however, was quite the most refreshing sporting narrative I ever listened to. This unlucky animal, the only one they had seen, floated alongside of the yacht on a cake of ice while they were at anchor in Bell Sound. Half the crew were absent in the whale-boat, which contained all the harpoons and lances; but Mr. Wood and two hands, armed with a rifle and a shotgun, valorously attacked the monster in the dingy. Unluckily, they only took two cartridges for the rifle; but they commenced proceedings by administering one of these to the walrus "*in his loins*," that naturally suggesting itself to them as being the most vulnerable part of the animal. It "seemed to go right through the walrus and disabled him, as he did not leave the ice, but merely raised his head and looked at them; upon which they gave him another bullet—in the head this time." I fancy this bullet must have struck the animal on the nostrils, as, upon receiving it, "he scuffled into the water, but could not remain underneath;" so they rowed after him, and continued firing repeated doses of *small shot* into his face whenever he appeared, until the persecuted amphibian went ashore, and, in the desperation of his heart, "walked back and forward" on the beach. There they thought they were sure of him; but he contrived to get past them, and finally sunk in deeper water. They then "swept" for him nearly a whole day with a weighted rope, but could not recover him.

An affair which might have had a termination any thing but comical, however, was, that they had burst the gun I had bought at Hammerfest for them to shoot fowls with. They seemed to attribute this catastrophe to the low price (four and a half dollars) which I had given for that weapon; but as a gentleman who accompanied me last summer had burst a seventy-guinea London rifle near the very same spot, a friend of mine burst a four-barrel the year before in Norway, and my present *compagnon de voyage*, Lord David Kennedy, burst another expensive rifle, by the same maker, a few years before in India, it seems that even the exorbitant prices charged by the *crack* London makers afford no security whatever against such accidents; so that I was inclined to attribute this mishap to careless loading. The explosion had very nearly deprived my valued sailing-master, Mr. Wood, of his left arm; and as it was, the arm had been burned and lacerated in a painful manner, but was now healing.

CHAPTER XV.

Bitter Cold.—Reindeer-shooting.—Three right and left Shots.—Delight of the Sailors.—Black Fox.—Ponche à la Spitzberg.—Description of the Reindeer.—High Condition he attains.—Excellence of his Flesh.—His Ignorance of Man.—Anecdotes.—Fine Valley.—Unexplored Channel.—Near Heinlopen Straits.—Unjust Attack.—Marrow-bones.—Ice-borne Boulders.—Good "Bag."—Two singular Mountains.—Thymen's Straits.—Meritorious Deer.—Receipt for Kabobs.—Splendid deer Forest.—Rejoin the Sloop.

By seven in the evening we had reached the anchorage opposite to a valley where I had killed some reindeer in 1858, but, it being Sunday, we did not land, nor was there any inducement to do so, as we could see the entire valley with telescopes from the deck, and there was not a single reindeer visible in it.

On the 25th we went ashore in both boats at 4 A.M. of a bitterly cold morning (thermometer 16° in the companion-way). After hauling the boats high and dry out of the reach of accidents, we ran about to warm ourselves, and then, taking different sides of a large wide valley, we proceeded to seek for deer. Lord David unluckily got among ground which had been hunted a few days previously (as we afterward ascertained) by a boat's crew from

Ericson's brig, and he consequently saw nothing, and returned to the yacht about midday.

I walked five or six miles, when I reached a high glen among the hills, and close to the line of perpetual snow and ice. It also snowed hard as we walked up, and it was frightfully cold, as the wind whistled down over the glaciers to the eastward of us. The walking, however, was excellent, as the intense frost had frozen the beastly, splashy, muddy, mossy compound which in Spitzbergen represents *soil* to the consistency of iron.

I first found three indifferent young deer on an open place where I could not approach nearer than 250 yards; but I managed to break the shoulder of the best one, and I finished him off with another shot. The other two ran up the glen in the mean time, and I did not follow them, as I now observed two much finer stags on a hill a mile off. I stalked up a little gully, which allowed me to approach quite close to these deer unseen by them; but the instant I put up my head to look at them they took the alarm, and were going best pace down a steep hill when my bullets overtook them, and they both rolled dead down the hill, going heels over head, like rabbits, as they fell.

My boat's crew now set to work to gralloch these deer, and to carry them down to the boat—half a deer to a man—while I followed up the glen in search of the two indifferent stags I had lost sight of. I found them about two miles up, and close to the edge of the glacier. They were not much alarmed, and had recommenced to feed, so I easily got within shot of them again, and I disposed of them also by a right and left shot. I opened these two deer myself, as the sailors were on their way to the boat. After having concluded this necessary but slightly disagreeable operation, I sat down and had a good look round with my glass. I soon had the satisfaction of discovering two superb stags lying down on the opposite side of the glen. It now began to snow very heavily, and under cover of it I crossed the glen, not far from the stags, without their seeing me. I got up to about a hundred yards or so from them, behind a bank of mossy earth, and shot one of them dead as he lay. The other sprang to his feet on hearing the report, and instantly shared a similar fate.

My sailors came back while I was admiring these two splendid stags as they lay bleeding on the snow, and loud were Jack's expressions of wonder, admiration, and delight at finding as many deer lying dead in the glen, after seven hours' stalking, as had taken them all four weeks to kill. One of these men—a fine young fellow, the very beau-ideal of an English sailor—was an ex-man-of-war's-man, and had assisted in that deplorable business at Petropaulauski, and he seemed to think that if they had had a few four-barreled rifles on that unhappy occasion, the Roosians would not have had so much the best of it!

REINDEER-SHOOTING.

I had now shot all the deer which I could discover in the valley, and more than my four sailors could carry down to the sea in one day. While we were cutting up the last two deer a black fox made his appearance, probably attracted by the smell of the venison; but he seemed to be fully aware of the important fact that his sable jacket was worth £20,* as he avoided all my attempts to get within rifle-shot of him.

Before proceeding to the sea with a second load of meat we ate some biscuits, and, as the intense frost had congealed all the water in this high valley, we indulged in a "*ponche à la Romaine*," or rather "*ponche à la Spitzberg*," by saturating cupfuls of snow with rum; and I can strongly recommend that cordial to any one under similar circumstances.

In this valley I observed some singular conical-shaped masses of *trap* or other Plutonic rock, which had abruptly burst up through the limestone hills.

We got on board about 4 P.M., and my four men having walked at least twenty miles, ten of which with half a fat stag on each of their backs, I sent a boat's crew of fresh hands to bring down the remainder of the venison.

The reindeer (*Cervus Tarandus*) abounds in most parts of Spitzbergen, and in every valley which af-

* A good skin of this rare animal is, I believe, the most valuable fur in the world.

fords any vegetation, a troop of from three to twenty is generally to be met with. They do not grow to such a large size as the tame reindeer of Lapland, nor are their horns quite so fine; but they attain to a most extraordinary degree of condition. This seems to be a sort of provision of nature to enable these animals to exist through the long Polar winter, as during that inclement season, although they no doubt obtain a little sustenance by picking the dry withered moss from spots which the wind has cleared of snow, as well as by scraping up the snow with their feet to get at it, still they must in a great measure subsist by consuming internally their own fat. The short space of time which suffices for them to lay on this coat of blubber is perfectly extraordinary; and as scarcely any grass exists even in the most favored parts of Spitzbergen, this must be chiefly attributable to some excessively nutritious properties in the mosses on which they feed. The deer killed by my yacht's crew in Bell Sound in July were mere skin and bone, whereas now, in the end of August, every deer we shot was *seal-fat*, and in all probability their condition goes on improving until the end of September. Of those we killed, even the hinds giving milk and the calves were very fat, and the old stags were perfectly obese, having all over their bodies a sort of cylinder of beautifully hard and white fat about two inches thick in most parts, and at least three inches thick over the haunches and on the brisket. We had no means of weighing these deer, but I consider that the best stags must have exceeded three hundred pounds in clean weight. I think the flesh of the reindeer is the richest and most delicious meat, wild or tame, which I ever tasted, with the exception of a fat eland, and a diminutive West Indian animal called by the negroes the Lapp* (*Cœlogenys*, or *Cavia Paca*). Unlike the flesh of most wild animals, the venison of the reindeer is not improved by keeping, and I think it is never better than the same day, or even the same hour, that the animal is killed. When it is kept long the fat gets dark colored, and acquires a rank and unpleasant taste and odor.

In the summer months they do not live in large herds together. An extensive valley may perhaps contain forty or fifty deer, but they are all in small independent companies of two, four, or six; and I have seldom, if ever, seen more than eight in one herd. In the winter season, however, when they come down to the islands and the wide flats on the sea-shore, I imagine they congregate in great numbers, and at that time they travel over long distances of ice and land in search of food.

The hair of the reindeer is very long, thick, and close, and is of a slaty-gray color, verging into white about the stern and belly. The hinds have horns

* After a somewhat extensive experience in that line, I am inclined to award to the Lapp the palm of being the best culinary animal in the world.

as well as the stags, although of a smaller size. They shed their horns every winter, and numbers of these cast horns strew the plains where the herds have wintered.

The deer I had killed on the 25th were reasonably shy and wild, as I think they had been hunted by Ericson's boat's crew in the lower valley a few days before; but sometimes they are incredibly tame and fearless, and I have repeatedly known deer, which I had failed in approaching unseen, to come up boldly of their own accord until they were within easy shot of me, although I was not only in full view, but to windward of them! I can only account for this extraordinary temerity on the part of these deer by supposing that they were individuals which had been reared in some remote part of the country, and had never seen a human being, *nor any thing else which could hurt them*,* in their previous blissful existences. Neither does the report of a rifle much alarm them; but that is more easily understood, as they are no doubt accustomed to hearing the cracking of the glaciers and the noises caused by the splitting of rocks from the frost in winter.

On one occasion Lord David Kennedy found a troop of five deer, and, obtaining a concealed posi-

* There are no wolves in Spitzbergen; and I am inclined to doubt whether the Polar bear ever meddles with the reindeer, unless he may fall in with a sick or wounded individual near the sea-shore.

tion within shot of them, he knocked over four of them with a round from his four-barreled rifle; the survivor then stood snuffing his dead companions until Kennedy had time to load one barrel, and to consummate this unparalleled sporting feat by polishing him off likewise.

Another time we broke one of the fore feet of an old fat stag from an unseen ambush; his companions ran away, and the wounded deer, after making some attempts to follow them, which the softness of the ground and his own corpulence prevented him from doing, looked about him a little, and then, seeing nothing, he actually began to graze on his three remaining legs as if nothing had happened of sufficient consequence to keep him from his dinner!

On the 26th, we again started at four in the morning in both boats, to make an expedition to the head of Stour Fiord, distant about seventeen miles, with the view of laying in a farther supply of deer. We first ran about six or seven miles under sail, with a fine breeze and smooth water; and then, the fiord making an abrupt turn to the east,* we were obliged to take to the oars, and after six hours of hard pulling against both wind and tide, we reached the *embouchure* of an extensive flattish valley, which I knew to be one of the best places in the country for deer. Here we left

* It is erroneously marked in the charts as if it continued straight north.

Lord David, as I felt sure that he would have no difficulty in filling his boat with venison. Not caring about that description of sport myself, I continued three or four miles farther on, to explore a sort of narrow gut or sound into which the fiord there contracts, in hopes of finding some floating ice with seals, or maybe a bear. We found a good deal of ice, but no seals; and, on entering the gut, there was such a tremendous current running down it that, after persevering for two or three miles more, we were obliged to stop.

I stopped with great reluctance, as I was extremely anxious to ascertain whether this channel really communicates with the East Sea or not. Many of the *habitués* of Spitzbergen believe that it does, but the point has never been clearly settled, as nobody has ever passed through the sound or seen the termination of it. I then tried to continue the exploration by walking up the sides of the sound; but the ground was so excessively rough as to be almost impracticable for walking, and I had to give it up.

Christian had been sixteen seasons in Spitzbergen, but he had never been so far up as this before, and could give me no information on the subject. He, however, agreed with me in opinion that there was strong evidence in favor of the communication being complete, because the water seemed very deep, and much heavy ice was floating down it; also, he thought the current was much stronger than was likely to be caused by the mere return of the regular tide down Stour Fiord.

The day was tolerably clear, but there was no hill near us on which we could ascend to obtain a more extended view in that direction. From the top of the highest rocks we could find we could see no high land to the eastward, nor any thing but low, flattish, rugged hillocks of a coarse red-brown Plutonic rock, with many small glaciers lying among them. The surface of these rocks was much smoothened and polished, as if by the passage over them of much heavy ice in by-gone times. There was not a particle of vegetation to be seen, and the aspect of the country was bleak, sterile, and gloomy beyond description.

Christian said the sky in that direction had the peculiar appearance which indicates ice underneath, and altogether our impression was that we were within a very few miles of the East Sea, probably at or about Heinlopen Straits. If the longitude of the coast of these straits is laid down in the charts at all correctly, we undoubtedly were close to them now; but the old charts of Spitzbergen are so extremely defective that no reliance is to be placed upon them in any respect.

I turned my back upon these unexplored straits with regret, and we now hoisted the sail and stood slowly along the coast of the main fiord to look for deer. In the first valley we came to we espied some small troops of deer feeding within half a mile of the shore. We landed, and I killed nine of them without much trouble, and, as these were thoroughly unsophisticated animals, I might easily have shot as many more, but I got disgusted with such a burlesque upon sport and left them alone. I was much amused by one of these deer—a well-grown stag—who, upon receiving my bullet in his ribs, made a furious attack upon a companion of about his own size, evidently under the impression that the bullet-wound was the result of a treacherous prod from the horns of his friend.

While the sailors were carrying down these deer I gathered a lot of drift-wood, and soon made a roaring fire, whereat we boiled some coffee and made a glorious fry of chops and kidneys in the iron baling-ladle of the boat, *topping up* with broiled marrow-bones—a very different article, O my dear reader, from the bestial compound of brains and lard rammed into old bones which you have often eaten in London, and imagined, in the innocence of your heart, to be *real marrow.*

When standing on the rocks up the small sound, I had observed a large bay on the opposite side of the fiord to be full of floating ice, and we now sailed across to that in hopes of falling in with seals. It was very suitable ice, but the night was too cold for seals, and we only found two on many square miles of ice. I shot them both, but one of them was lost. I observed a great many large, dark-colored stones lying on different pieces of this ice, and mistook several of them for seals, until we got close enough to discover our mistake. These stones probably tumbled off the hills on the ice while it lay in an unbroken sheet across the fiord, and were now being transported about to be deposited elsewhere.

We had a cold and fatiguing row back to the yacht, and did not reach her until we had been twenty-eight hours absent.

As I expected, Lord David had found his valley full of deer, and had shot a boat-load of them. His men had farther to carry them than mine had, so they did not reach the yacht until after an absence of nearly forty hours.

I observed two very singular mountains in this trip up the high fiord. One of these was a long, large hill of about 1500 feet in height, and apparently composed of the same shaly, sandy limestone as mostly all of the lower hills of East Spitzbergen; but it had a perfectly flat or tabular top, and the upper stratum, as well as another band about the middle of the hill, were composed of black substance, which I supposed to be coal. I was not within several miles of the hill, but I estimated the thickness of each of these black bands at about twenty feet. Their substance was evidently pretty hard, as the ends of the bands stood up perpendicularly, instead of participating in the otherwise uniform 45° slope of the hill. At the left-hand or southwesterly side of the hill I could perceive that the lower band gradually thinned away to nothing. This hill is very conspicuously placed, and can not fail to be recognized by any future visitor to the upper part of Stour Fiord.

The other hill I imagine to be a truncated cone of Plutonic rock, and of it I can hardly hope to give a sketch that will convey any idea of its singularly grand and picturesque appearance. It seemed to be about 600 feet high, and two or three miles in circumference at the base; and the lower two thirds of its height consisted of a steep *talus* of detritus, covered with beautifully variegated mosses, while the upper third was composed of a series of bright russet-colored columns of rock, arranged perpendicularly, and looking exactly like a number of half-decayed trunks of enormous trees bound together in a sort of Titanic fagot.

27*th*. After myself and my boat's crew had had five hours' sleep, we started again on another trip, my intention being to penetrate well into Walter Thymen's Straits, a narrow passage of twenty or five-and-twenty miles long and five or six in breadth, which divides East Spitzbergen into two nearly equal halves.

When there is ice in this strait it is a great *thoroughfare* for seals and sea-horses passing from the East Sea into Stour Fiord, and we were in hopes that ice would by this time have been driven into it by the current from the east. It is considered a dangerous place for vessels, on account of the violent current running through it; so I preferred going in the boat to risking my yacht itself in the straits.

It seemed by the chart as if we had not more than ten or twelve miles to go, as in the chart there is laid down at the northwest corner of the straits what appears to be a bank with shallow water over it, protruding a long way into Stour Fiord. We had a fine day, with a strong, though bitterly cold breeze of east wind, and I steered the boat close along shore, hoping, as it was near high tide, that we might have sufficient depth of water to enable us to make a short cut by sailing over this bank. On reaching the edge of the bank, however, I found, to my surprise, that it was not a submarine bank at all, but an immense flat plain of dry land, edged with a reef of rocks several feet above high tide mark, and we had to make a long detour to get round it.

As there has been no survey of Spitzbergen in recent times, and all the charts are copied from an ancient Dutch or Danish one, published two centuries or more ago, I think it is highly probable that this point of land was actually under water (as the chart seems to represent it) at the time the latter was constructed, and that it has since been gradually elevated to its present level. Enormous quantities of drift-wood lay upon the reef of rocks above the sea-level.

When we had got round this long promontory

and about six miles into the straits it fell calm, and we encountered such a strong current from the eastward that we could make no head against it, and, it being now 9 P.M., we went ashore in a little sandy bay to spy out the land, and see whether it afforded any thing for supper. I took my rifle and my glass, and ascended to the top of a neighboring hillock, and from there I soon discovered our evening meal provided to our hands in the shape of a fat stag, grazing by himself on the slope of a hill about a mile distant. I therefore announced to the crew that we should sup there, and set two of them to gather wood and make a fire, while the other two accompanied me to carry down the stag, who was still quietly engaged with *his own* supper, and in a happy state of unconsciousness of how soon he would be called upon to conjugate the verb *to sup* in a passive instead of an active sense.

A beautifully developed terrace of trap rocks conducted me within forty yards of the stag, and in twenty minutes more he was at the side of the fire, which, like those of the cannibals in Robinson Crusoe, had been lighted for him while yet alive.

I shudder to think how many pounds of this meritorious animal we consumed in the shape of chops, marrow-bones, and *kabobs*. The latter I have found on such occasions to be the best mode of cooking fresh-killed meat. The mode of preparing them is as follows:

First catch a fat deer, then cut a number of

wooden skewers, and thread upon these alternately pieces of meat, fat, and heart, each cut to about the size and thickness of a dollar; broil upon the glowing embers, season with wood-ashes in the absence of salt and pepper, and bite them off while smoking hot. If you are hungry, you fancy this the most delicious thing you ever tasted. For my knowledge of this most interesting *plat* I was indebted to a one-eyed Arab cook, yclept Hadji Mohammed, whom Sir F—— S—— and myself had on an expedition in Egypt and Palestine some years ago. I have also seen kabobs retailed to the faithful by itinerant cooks in the streets of Constantinople.

After supper we erected a screen to windward of the fire by hanging the boat's sail upon the harpoon shafts; and then, lighting our pipes, we lay down to sleep on the beach, "Plenus Bacchi,* pinguisque ferinæ," like the pious Æneas and his companions on the shores of Italia.

We have lost sight of the midnight sun for the last few days, and it was slightly dusk at night. The temperature was far below frost, but we slept very comfortably. The crew kept watch alternately, to mind the boat and keep up the fire, and I could observe, in my waking moments, that the sentinel always seemed to be whiling away the tedious hours by renewed attacks upon the carcass of the stag.

* For "Bacchi" read "backy," and the quotation will be more applicable.

On awaking in the morning, I summoned one of the men to my assistance, and walked to a place about half a mile distant, where, when stalking the stag the evening before, I had observed some bones of a whale protruding from the moss at a good elevation. The height above the sea proved to be about forty-two feet, and the entire skeleton of a very large whale lay there partially imbedded in moss and earth. There was a terrace of trap rocks between it and the sea, higher in most places than the ground where the bones lay. These were a good deal decayed, and were now frozen hard to the ground, but we managed to extract a piece of a jaw-bone,* tolerably sound, and as large as a man could carry.

I sent my attendant back to the boat with this trophy, and I walked to the top of a steep hill, to have a good look along the straits, to see if there was no appearance of the eastern ice coming through. From the height I was on, I must have seen nearly to the east end of the straits; but they seemed quite clear of ice throughout their entire length. There were two considerable glaciers some miles down the straits, one on each side, and both protruding into the sea.

For several miles about me, both to the east and west, there extended the most beautiful piece of country, to the eye of a deer-stalker, which I ever beheld. To the east there lay a low flat plain,

* Now in the Museum of the Geological Society.

green with succulent mosses, and not less than ten thousand acres in extent; this plain gradually contracted in breadth, until below where I stood, it was only about a mile broad between the hills and the straits, and here it was intersected with dry water-courses, and ridges, and dikes of trap rocks, affording admirable stalking-ground. From the plain up to the rocky hill whereon I stood was a slope or talus, beautifully carpeted with mosses; before me stretched a level plateau, or table-land, and above that a number of grand sheltered corries, with high rugged mountains towering over all. The frost was intense, but the sun shining brightly, the plains and the rocky slopes looked as if covered with a brilliant Turkey carpet, being red, brown, green, yellow, orange, and purple with mosses. The whole scene made up such a picture, or beau-ideal of a deer-forest as I never saw before.

I did not care about shooting any more deer now, and there seemed to be no chance of that much more exciting quarry, the sea-horse, so we prepared to start. Before leaving the yacht the day before, I had told Mr. Wood to get up his anchor as soon as Lord David should return on board, and drop down to a well-known anchorage at the southeast corner of the straits, and I would meet him there; but now, as there was nothing to be done in the straits with the walruses, and we had *tons* of venison on board, I determined to intercept the yacht, and prevent her from coming to an anchor. When we saw from the heights, therefore, that the yacht was coming down, we made sail to meet her.

Soon after we started, we saw six or seven cakes of ice in a small bay, where they were kept together by a sort of eddy, and upon one of these lay a big seal asleep. I shot him and took him with us; but when we got on board the yacht, I was astonished to find that it was Sunday, a fact of which I had previously been quite unaware.

We sailed rapidly down the fiord, and joined our consort off Hvalfiske Point in the evening.

CHAPTER XVI.

Dead Walrus found.—Bears nearly escape, but are caught.—Gale and Ice.—Mynherr Holmengreen.—Presents *more Kaffirorum*.—Send home the Sloop.—Result of Ericson's eight Months' Voyage.—South Cape.—Sugar-loaf Mountain.—"Right Whales."—Parasitical Gulls.—Practical Joke.—Arctic Fauna.—Chain of Subsistence.—Divergence of White Bear from original Stock.—Probable Origin of the Walrus.—And of the Seal.—Of the Cetaceans.—Changes in the South African Antelopes, caused by Desiccation of that country.

THE "Anna Louisa's" people had also killed a few reindeer on the extensive plains near the Russian huts; and they had found a bull-walrus floating dead in the water, and of course added his blubber to the cargo. He was probably one of those we had shot and sunk. I believe they all float up after a few days, but the currents are so strong that they are swept away to sea, and are very rarely recovered.

The young bears had made a most determined effort to escape, and had very nearly succeeded. One day, while all hands except the cook were ashore, they had taken the opportunity to eat through the rotten drift-wood composing their cage, and to break out on deck. The cook, hearing the scuffling of their feet, came up and attempted to drive them in again, but they completely got the better of him, and compelled him to make a precipitate retreat to the masthead for security. They then added insult to injury, and still farther embittered the cook's feelings by devouring great part of a haunch of fat venison which was hanging on deck ready for dinner. Finally, and we may suppose after a facetious grin at the cook aloft, they clambered over the side and swam ashore. Their triumph, however, was not of long duration, for the rest of the crew accidentally met them coolly traveling along the shore in the evening; and although at first they were nearly shooting them for wild bears, at last it occurred to them, from there being no old one with them, that they were their young shipmates trying to escape; so they pursued and recaptured them, but not until after a most severe struggle, in the course of which one or two of the men got severely bitten by the young demons, who had now grown much too big and strong to be handled with impunity.

We determined to have one more last look at the edge of the main ice pack to the northeast, as the weather was so fine that we thought we might still pick up a sea-horse or two. Both yacht and sloop sailed in company at midnight, steering for Black Point. A howling gale of northeasterly wind came on early in the morning, but the "Ginevra," in which we still continued, easily beat up against it, and got close to Black Point about 10 A.M. on the 29th. We found great quantities of ice had come down, and long lines of it stretched far away to the south of us.

Near Black Point we recognized Danielsen's schooner, and another small vessel from Bergen, commanded by one Mynherr Holmengreen. They were both at anchor, in shelter of an island to leeward of the ice; and as it was blowing much too hard for boat work, we dropped anchor beside them.

Mynherr Danielsen, probably observing the long rows of fat quarters of venison hung up in our rigging, honored us with an immediate call. He said his vessel, with Holmengreen's and our two, were now the only remaining ships in the Spitzbergen seas. He had been looking for walruses on the Thousand Islands for ten days past; but had got nothing except one of our dead ones. The Bergen schooner had found a herd of several hundreds on one of these islands; but the men most indiscreetly attacked them to windward, and the walruses taking the alarm, all rushed into the sea. This must have been the more provoking for the unlucky schooner, as they had only killed fifteen all summer.

Mr. Holmengreen also called to pay his respects to us—or our venison; and we were much surprised to find him a stout, well-dressed, benevolent-looking, elderly party in a brown wig! Altogether he had much more the appearance of a well-to-do London merchant than a Spitzbergen walrus-hunter; and yet this man is said to be one of the pluckiest and most skillful harpooners who ever transfixed a walrus.

In the afternoon my steward informed me, with a very serious air indeed, that we were "quite out of sugar," and he suggested that it would be a "good plan to *borrow* some from the schooners;" so I sent the captains each four fat quarters of deer, and desired one of our harpooners, who carried the meat, to say, with my compliments, that if they had any sugar to spare, it would be an acceptable return for the gift, as we were quite out of that luxury. This was somewhat in the Kaffir fashion of making presents, and Johann seemed to think it was to be a literal case of barter; for he said to me, "I suppose, if they have got no sugar, then I will bring back the deer?" I replied, "Of course not; give the deer, and then ask for some sugar." Nor was my confidence misplaced, for they sent us enough sugar to last us to Hammerfest, and the mind of Mr. Quirk, the steward, was set at rest.

30*th*. It still blows very hard from north-north-east, with heavy snow. Thermometer is about 28°, and barometer very low.

The "Anna Louisa" joined us last night.

In the evening it looked no better. The barometer *would not* rise, and the ice began to sweep round us; so Mr. Wood said that he must get the yacht at all events out of this anchorage before next tide, as she had received some very severe bangs from heavy icebergs already; and, not being protected by exterior planking, like the other three vessels, it would not do to expose her to such risk any more. We held a council of war, and discussed three alternatives which we had before us:

First: We might shift again into the sloop, and obstinately ride out the gale in her, and then, if it abated within a few days, we might hope for three or four days more at the walruses, if we could find any. In this case the yacht must be sent away in charge of a pilot to await us at South Cape, or elsewhere, clear of the ice. One grave objection to this course was, that if thick weather came on we might not be able to find the yacht at sea, and there was no harbor in which I would now trust her nearer than Ice Fiord, as Horn Sound and Bell Sound are liable to be choked up in one night when the ice is moving fast round to the westward.

Second: We could go home to Hammerfest "holus-bolus," as Mr. Wood expressed it, and,

Third: We could send the sloop over to Hammerfest, and go round to Ice Fiord ourselves in the yacht for a few days. The advantages of the last plan were that the sloop's crew could be paid off, and our cargo valued and accounts squared by the time that we should probably arrive, and that we might thus escape the chance of detention in Hammerfest. We were also assured of getting plenty of reindeer, and maybe white whales, in Ice Fiord; but as that part of the coast is clear of ice in the autumn, we must bid good-by to the sea-horses for this season.

After some deliberation, we decided on adopting the last-mentioned plan, and it seemed to give general satisfaction to all concerned, including the masters of the two schooners, who were resolved to remain to the last, and therefore appeared to think that our terrible rifles would be well out of their way.

In an hour after making up our minds we had got all our things out of the sloop, "liquored-up" the crew of the latter, written a letter to our agents in Hammerfest, got the boats stowed, the anchors up, and made sail, we for South Cape, and the "Anna Louisa" for Hammerfest. We still kept Johann and Christian in the yacht to act as pilots and harpooners.

The "Anna Louisa" carried with her a man belonging to Hammerfest, who had been a harpooner in Ericson's brig. Ericson had left him on board the "Anna Louisa" at Hvalfiske Point, with a letter for me, in which he expressed a hope that I would give him a passage to Hammerfest, as it would save the expense and delay of sending him by steam-boat from Tonsberg, in the south of Norway, to Hammerfest, in the extreme north. The man thus luckily avoided a voyage of about 3000 miles.

Poor Ericson has a pretty wife with a young family in Tonsberg, and he must have gone home to her with a heavy heart, for he has made but a bad summer's "fishing" of it. Between Jan Mayen and Spitzbergen, he has been away from home seven months; and his letter to me mentions that he has only killed 270 Jan Mayen seals, 140 big Spitzbergen seals, 62 walruses, 4 bears, and 35 reindeer; a cargo which will afford but a miserable remuneration for eight* months' time of a brig carrying twenty-four men, and constantly manning four boats, and five upon an emergency.

31*st.* Early in the morning we are off South Cape, the sea quite free from ice and the weather fine. I think storms are very *local* in Spitzbergen, and it is probably as coarse as ever at Black Point, that stormy promontory where we encountered so many fierce gales of wind.

Very long, low, and dangerous reefs of rocks run out many miles from the land all along the coast, from South Cape to Ice Fiord. The mountains are much higher and steeper than in East Spitzbergen. There is one enormous sugar-loaf-looking peak, not far from South Cape. It appears to be of granite, and is said to be the highest mountain in Spitzbergen. This is evidently the mountain described by Scoresby, who states its height to be 4500 feet; although, judging by the eye, I should have estimated it at considerably more.

* Allowing one month to reach Tonsberg.

Many of these mountains have a singularly striking resemblance, on an enormously exaggerated scale, to the pyramids of Egypt. Some of them have four well-proportioned sides, and slope at a very regular angle of about 45° from top to bottom; and the lines of stratification being very horizontally disposed and broken short off at the ends, give them exactly the appearance of being composed of gigantic courses of masonry, each smaller than the one below it, until the mountain terminates in an absolute point. Others, again, have the uppermost strata slightly overhanging, or projecting over those immediately below.

The 1st of September was a fine calm day, with only occasional gusts of wind from the valleys on the coast.

We saw two huge Mysticeti, or "right whales," lazily rolling on the surface and blowing sonorously, at one or two miles' distance. They remained so long above water after each dive that it looked as if there would be no great difficulty in harpooning them, and only our want of proper tackle compelled us reluctantly to abstain from making the experiment.

The sea here swarms with incredible numbers of minute Medusæ, on which these whales were probably feeding when we saw them. These animalculæ also seem to be affording an inexhaustible banquet to gulls and guillemots by the thousand. The latter are the only things we ever take the lives of without intending to make any use of them afterward; but they afford such admirable marks for rifle practice, that the slaughter of them is perhaps justifiable, as affording a means to the end.

It is very amusing to watch the proceedings of the parasitical gulls, of whom two or three species exist here—*Larus parasiticus* and *Larus glaucus;* the latter is called by the Dutchmen the "Burgomaster," from his tyrannical and rapacious selfishness. Neither of these birds ever seem to take the trouble to pick up any thing for themselves; but as soon as they observe any other gull in possession of a morsel which he is not able to swallow outright, they dash at him and hunt him through the air, until the victim is obliged to drop whatever he has secured, and the ravenous burgomaster then appropriates and swallows it himself. I have watched many of these nefarious transactions, and the result is always the same; the small gull turns, and twists, and doubles, and dodges, screaming all the time so pitifully that one would think he expected to lose his life instead of his dinner; but at last he is compelled to give up possession, and the burgomaster then ceases to molest him. In the breeding season, these parasitical gulls also pick the eggs out of the nests of the inferior tribes; but, fortunately for the latter, the number of their persecutors is very limited, or else they would soon get exterminated altogether, and then *L. parasiticus* and *L. glaucus* would be compelled to have recourse to a more reputable mode of life to obtain a subsistence.

The sailors are very fond of playing off a certain practical joke on the gulls which are always hovering about the ships. The trick is this: you take three or four pieces of sail-twine, of a fathom or so in length, tie them all together in the middle, and to the end of each tightly attach a small piece of blubber, then throw the whole into the sea; a gull comes and swallows one piece; another then sees there is plenty to spare, and swallows the next; perhaps a third gull takes possession of another; but as they are all attached to one another by the sail-yarns, whenever they try to fly away, one party or another is perforce compelled to disgorge his share; and this is continued at the expense of the poor gulls alternately, to the great amusement of the sailors.

It seems to me that an attentive study of the Arctic *Fauna* is capable of throwing great light upon some debated questions in Natural History.

I am aware that I am now treading upon very dangerous ground, and that what I say will be severely criticised; but I will "take a header" into the deep waters of controversy at once, and unhesitatingly avow my belief that an attentive study of the Arctic animals is capable of mightily strengthening the theory of *progressive development*, first suggested by the illustrious Lamarck, and since so ably expounded and defended, under somewhat modified forms, by the author of the "Vestiges of Creation," and by Mr. Charles Darwin.

There, *Messieurs les Critiques*, is a chance for you! "Pitch into him; jump down his throat; tear him to pieces; the Atheist! the Lamarckian! the disciple of the atrocious author of the 'Vestiges,'" etc., etc., etc.

I acknowledge with humility my presumption in entering upon so profound a question in Natural History; but, although I make no pretensions to the character of a scientific naturalist, still I have had opportunities such as few have enjoyed, of observing and studying the habits and mode of life of strange animals in many strange countries; and the more I observe nature, and ponder on the subject, the more do I become convinced that Almighty God always carries out his intentions with regard to the animal creation, *not* by "direct interpositions" of His will, nor by "special fiats of creation," but by the slow and gradual agency of natural causes.

It might naturally be expected that in such inclement regions, and where so little vegetation exists as in the Arctic zone, there must only be very few living animals, and those few of a dwarfish and miserable nature; but, on the contrary no portion of the surface of the globe more abounds in animal life, from the minute animalculæ—which, although too small to be seen in detail without a microscope, are yet in the aggregate so numberless as to discolor the ocean—to the huge walrus and the vast mysticetus with his congeners. All this life hangs together from link to link in a beautiful chain: thus the different animalculæ prey on one another; the shrimps and small fishes prey on the larger animalculæ; the seals and walruses and the numerous sea-fowl prey on the shrimps and the fishes; the bear preys on the seal and the walrus, and the fox on the sea-fowl.

The Polar bear seems to me to be nothing more than a variety of the bears inhabiting Northern Europe, Asia, and America; and it surely requires no very great stretch of imagination to suppose that this variety was originally created, not as we see him now, but by individuals of *Ursus arctos* in Siberia, who, finding their means of subsistence running short, and pressed by hunger, ventured on the ice and caught some seals. These individuals would find that they could make a subsistence in this way, and would take up their residence on the shore, and gradually take to a life on the ice. Polar bears in the present day are often carried on the ice to Iceland, and even to within swimming distance of Northern Norway, so there is no impossibility in supposing that the brown bears, who by my theory were the progenitors of the present white bears, were accidentally driven over to Greenland and Spitzbergen by storms or currents. Individual bears of *U. arctos* are found frequently of *a silvery gray* color, and such bears are known in

Norway as "silver bears." Then it stands to reason that those individuals who might happen to be palest in color would have the best chance of succeeding in surprising seals, and those who had most external fat would have the best chance of withstanding the cold. The process of natural selection would do the rest, and *Ursus arctos* would, in the course of a few thousands, or a few millions of years, be transformed into the variety at present known as *Ursus maritimus.*

It may be urged against this that "there is no reason, if my theory is true, why brown bears are not still occasionally taking to a Polar life, catching seals and turning white" (?) The answer is easy; the ground is already occupied by the variety of bear formed by Nature, acting through the process of natural selection, for catching seals. The seals are so shy that even the existing white bears have difficulty in living, and a brown bear, although he may eke out his means of subsistence by occasionally still catching a seal on the shores of Siberia, would have no chance of succeeding in the struggle for life if he were to set off on a seal-hunting expedition, and to enter into competition with his white congeners, who are already formed and fitted by Nature, through countless generations, for that particular mode of life.*

* It will be obvious to any one that I follow Mr. Darwin in these remarks; and although the substance of this chapter was written in Spitzbergen, before the "Origin of Species" was

I think the appearance and the very existence of the *walrus* are among the strongest and most incontestable proofs to be found in the handwriting of Nature throughout all the animal kingdom in support of the theory of creation by slow and gradual causes, and in opposition to that of abrupt, unnatural, and uncalled-for interpositions of the Divine will.

There are very few or no animals in the world which seem to me to constitute so clear and well-defined *a link* between two different and distinct races; and I can hardly understand how any reflecting and unprejudiced person can attentively study the habits of the walrus when alive, or even attentively examine his skeleton when dead, without coming to the conclusion that he forms a plain and unmistakable link between animals inhabiting the land and the cetaceans or whales.

The *origin* of the walrus is a much more difficult and complicated problem to solve than to account for the divergence from the original stock of the white bear; but, nevertheless, I think the walrus must have originated in much the same sort of way as that by which I have attempted to explain the origin of *U. maritimus;* only, for the creation

published, I do not claim any originality for my views; and I also cheerfully acknowledge that, but for the publication of that work in connection with the name of so distinguished a naturalist, I never would have ventured to give to the world my own humble opinions on the subject.

of the walrus I must claim the indulgence of my opponents to grant me a few more millions of that *cheapest of all commodities, past years.* I require this little extension to enable me to make good my argument, because the walrus differs far more from any known animal, living or extinct, than does the white from the brown bear; also, I have stated that I conceive the Polar bear to have *become* a Polar bear by living on seals, and it is therefore to be supposed that the seal and the walrus were originated *first.*

In reference to the fact of a black bear having been seen swimming for hours with his mouth open, catching insects in the water, like a whale, Mr. Darwin states (page 174) that, "Even in so extreme a case as this, if the supply of insects were constant, and if better adapted competitors did not already exist in the country, he can see no difficulty in a race of bears being rendered by natural selection more and more aquatic in their structure and habits, with larger and larger mouths, till a creature was produced as monstrous as a whale."

I see no difficulty in it either, but it is certainly a very extreme case to put, and there is much less difficulty in believing that the thing should have come to pass in a more gradual manner—by steps, as it were.

Suppose, then, the case of a bear (*or* any *other large land animal, existing or extinct*) living on the borders of the then existing Polar sea. We can easily fancy that in the struggle for existence perpetually going on, this bear—or whatever he was—may have been compelled to take to the sea-shore and prey upon shell-fish among other things. At first he would only go into shallow water, but he would become emboldened, by success and habit, to go deeper and deeper; even in the lifetime of one individual this would happen, and he would acquire the habit of digging shells up with his feet or his teeth—at first probably with his feet, but latterly, when he came to picking shells in a foot or two of water, he would require to see what he was about, and he would use his teeth. Natural selection would now come into play, and as those animals which had the best and longest teeth would succeed best, so they would have the best chance of transmitting these peculiarities to their descendants. The tusks of the walrus are not, as I mentioned before, a pair of extra teeth, but merely an enlargement or extraordinary development of the eye-teeth, and I think it is easy to conceive that any large carnivorous animal, driven by necessity to subsist on shell-fish under water, would, in a few thousands of generations, acquire such tusks.

Also, he would soon learn to dive,* and to hold his breath under water, and from generation to generation he would be able to stay longer below. As he would have very little use for his legs, they

* I stated, *antè*, that we had seen the white bear dive for a short distance just like a walrus.

would soon become abortive *as legs*, and grow more into the resemblance of *fins;* the hind legs would somewhat resemble the tail of a fish, and would do duty for that organ; so his real tail would almost disappear, as is the case with the seal and the walrus.

The legs of the walrus, although almost abortive, are still legs, and not fins, as *he can walk on all four* on land or ice. Those of the seal are more abortive still, and the latter can not walk, strictly speaking, but only jerk himself along. Nobody who has seen the anatomy of a whale's paddles can deny that even they are legs and not fins, although, of course, only used to propel him in the water after the manner of fins.

The resemblance between the seal and the walrus is not in any respect so close, either in their appearance or in their habits, as one would be apt to suppose by looking at the clumsily stuffed specimen of a walrus in the British Museum, or at the few absurd caricatures of this animal which exist. The walrus in every way partakes much more of the nature of land animals than the seal, which again seems more closely allied to the cetaceans. For instance, the walrus can double his hind legs under him and walk upon them like any other beast, while the seal always keeps his hinder extremities stretched backward like the tail of a cetacean. The walrus can not remain under water for nearly so long a period as the seal, neither can he sustain the pressure of the water at any thing like the depth to which the great seal can descend: the walrus goes ashore on the beach or rocks, and the Spitzbergen seal, although he basks *on ice*—both fixed and floating—is never known to go on land or even to lie on a half-tide rock; the walrus is gregarious and the great seal solitary, even two seldom being found together; the young walrus lives with his dam for two seasons,* while the young seals are believed to leave the protection of the old ones at a few days old, and to shift for themselves like young fishes. I believe a young seal is never found along with its dam. The food of the walrus is chiefly obtained by plowing the submarine banks with his tusks, and the seal catches his prey swimming in the water.

This evidence would seem to argue that the seal is a farther intermediate link between the walrus and the whale, but I can not presume to hazard any opinion on that point; he may have diverged from the walrus, or he may have sprung more directly from some other race of animals living or extinct, without the intervention of the walrus.

But, in whatsoever way the numerous tribes of seals may have originated, I think that we have strong evidence before us, in the appearance and habits of the great seal and the walrus, to induce us to entertain the belief that one or other of them,

* We always found one-year-old calves with their mothers, *i. e.* calves of the preceding season.

or some allied animal now extinct, has been the progenitor of the whales and other cetaceans.

It is needless to recapitulate the description of the manner in which I humbly conceive it possible that these mighty animals might have been developed, as the cases hypothetically put before must have explained my meaning sufficiently; and my utmost hope is that the suggestions and remarks I have thrown out about the appearance and habits of animals so little known may assist in enabling other better qualified advocates of the great theory of *progressive development by means of natural selection* to work it out to demonstration.

This is not a treatise on Natural History, but a narrative of a summer's sporting trip in the Arctic regions, and I have only alluded to this intricate subject in its connection with the curious animals I have described, or I could easily fill a volume with facts corroborative of my views, taken from my own observations of many other animals in widely different parts of the earth. I will content myself with *one*.

In a district of South Africa, not larger than Britain, and not extending beyond ten degrees of latitude, there are well known to exist nearly *thirty varieties* of antelopes, from the huge eland of six feet in height and 2000 lbs. in weight to the diminutive bluebuck of 8 lbs. or 9 lbs. weight and twelve inches high.

Some of these varieties are confined to a particular range of rocky mountains, the banks of a particular river, or a particular series of flats; in other places as many as six varieties may be seen at one *coup d'œil*, and as many as ten or twelve in the course of a morning's ride. Of several varieties which inhabit the vast Kalahari Desert, some do not drink above once in three or four days, and others are never known to drink *at all*. The whole of these antelopes, although differing more or less in size, color, shape, horns, and habits, have strong points of resemblance to one another, first in groups or classes, and then altogether. Some of them are so nearly alike to another variety that no two people, either among naturalists or among the colonists and inhabitants, seem to be agreed whether these very similar varieties constitute separate species or not.

Now, will any man attempt to make me believe that *each and all* of these numerous varieties (or species) of antelopes were originally brought into being separately and distinctly as we see them now? That one variety was specially created for this petty locality, and another for that? That there was a special interposition of Providence to create a variety about the outskirts of the desert, which should only drink water once in three or more days, and other varieties which should be absolute non-drinkers?

I think reflection and an attentive observation of nature lead one to a very different conclusion.

Dr. Livingstone has shown that vast portions of South Africa, which formerly used to be well-watered, have been for long, and still are, undergoing a rapid desiccation,* and it seems to me that that important fact alone is sufficient to account for many of these antelopes having changed their peculiarities and habits; and with the latter, through the lapse of countless ages, their size, shape, color, horns, and other distinctions. Nay, farther, I entertain no doubt that they are undergoing these said changes *at this moment*, but by such a slow and gradual process that it is quite imperceptible in the brief space of human life, or even within the period since natural history began to be studied.

A chapter might easily be here written about that singular animal, the wildebeeste, or gnu, which seems to be a tolerably well-defined link between the antelopes and the bovine tribe; but I will now leave the discussion of the subject to abler pens than mine.

* My own personal observation in South Africa abundantly confirms that remark of the doctor's.

R

CHAPTER XVIII.

Horn and Bell Sounds.—Ice Fiord.—Pickled Reindeer's Tongues.—Arctic Foxes.—Geology.—Raised Beaches.—Fossil Cannon-balls.—Awful Avalanche.—Begins to get dark at Night.—Reach Hammerfest.—Sell our Cargo.—Take Leave of our Crew.—Sail home.—Equinoctial Gales.—Leith.—"Glut" of Bears in the British Market.—Conclusion.—Game List.

On passing the mouth of Horn Sound, we encountered a tremendous blast of wind blowing out of that fiord as out of a funnel. This helped us for a little, and then it fell almost calm again until we came opposite to the entrance of Bell Sound, where we experienced just such another squall from the northeast.

Going close-hauled, it was as much as the yacht could do to stand up against it under close-reefed mainsail, foresail, and staysail; but this squall carried us nearly to the mouth of Ice Fiord, where these gusts of wind blowing down through the high valleys were more violent than ever, and were now accompanied with heavy sleety rain. We beat up the fiord in the teeth of this, and anchored in a sheltered bay in the evening of the 2d.

The sporting season seemed to be about come to an end; but we were now obliged to stop here for

GROUP OF REINDEER.

a few days to fill the water-tanks, and gather fire-wood enough for the return voyage. There is no danger in remaining here for at least a week or two to come, as this is said to be the last harbor in Spitzbergen which remains open. The reason for this is that the stream coming round from the east here encounters that portion of the Arctic current which sweeps round the northwest corner of Spitzbergen, and runs through the channel between Prince Charles' Island and the main land.

Immense flights of geese, both of the gray and brent varieties, winging their way to the south, warn us, however, that it is nearly time to leave the regions of the ice.

In the numerous fine valleys entering from Ice Fiord we found such quantities of reindeer that we might have loaded the ship with them, if we had been, in the language of "Bell's Life," "*gluttons*" for that description of sport; but, as we had more venison on board than all hands, including the young bears, could eat in a month, we contented ourselves by picking out a few of the old stags with the best horns we could find.

The tongues of the reindeer are particularly delicious, and we salted a small keg of these for distribution among our friends at home.

We have now secured splendid specimens of all the Spitzbergen animals worthy of a sportsman's attention, except the narwhal and the black fox. These are both very rare, and we never had the satisfaction of adding the long spiral horn of the one, or the beautiful skin of the other, to our collections.

On a promontory of sandy beach near our anchorage there were always a lot of gulls resting, and a small white fox, apparently half mad with hunger, continued the whole day making unavailing efforts to *stalk* them. He would go away for half an hour until he thought the gulls might have gone to sleep, and then come sneaking back to try it again; but the gulls were always too wide awake for him.

There are a great many foxes on this part of Spitzbergen, and it is rather a curious subject to speculate upon how they subsist in winter? All the geese and eider-ducks, and I should imagine also the gulls, leave Spitzbergen in September. There are no hares or other small land animals, and the occasional windfall of a dead deer or seal can surely not maintain the foxes for seven or eight months out of the twelve. Do they then hibernate like the Norway bear, or lay up a secret store of sea-fowl and eggs against the winter? If the latter, it is one of the most singular cases of instinct sharpened by necessity to be found in nature.

There are several well-developed raised beaches around some parts of Ice Fiord. In one place I observed three of these, each one about eight or ten feet above the other.

Nothing strikes a geological observer in Spitzbergen more than the total absence of *pebbly beaches.* I was especially requested by a distinguished geologist to direct my attention to this matter, and I did so; but I nowhere saw, on any part of the coast between Ryk Yse Islands and Ice Fiord, nor among the Thousand Islands, any thing approaching to what can be called a pebbly beach. Nine tenths of the coast consists of glacier, rocks, and clay. In some places there are bays with sandy beaches, and in others I have observed great accumulations of coarse rhomboidal gravel, both on the beach and at different elevations, but I never saw a beach composed of rounded, water-worn pebbly stones on any part of the coasts of Spitzbergen.

The mountains about this fiord are composed of a friable, crumbling limestone, which in great part has a sort of brown tinge, as if impregnated with oxide of iron. They are perfectly chock-full of fossils, so much so as to look as if they were actually composed of fossils in some places. I gathered many specimens, and I also picked up, in the bed of a torrent, three stones so exactly spherical, and so highly ferruginous-looking, that my Petropaulauski man-of-war's-man stoutly maintained that if the "other stones" I gave him to carry were the fossils of clams and cockles, these must undoubtedly be the *fossils of cannon-shot* of different calibres.

There is a good walrus-boat lying on the beach in a small bay here. This boat was found two years ago floating bottom up, and with two of the harpoon-lines broken, from which it is concluded that a walrus had upset her and drowned the crew.

On the fourth, while we were busy on deck making preparations to depart, we saw a tremendous avalanche of rocks, ice, and earth descend from the face of a steep mountain three or four miles distant. I should think the mass consisted of several millions of tons, and the terrific roar and splash with which it descended into the sea baffle all attempts at description. It is fortunate we were not anchored underneath it at the time.

We got the two heavy boats in on deck, and secured them firmly in case of bad weather, and made every thing else as *snug* as possible for the return voyage.

We have some difficulty in stowing the venison, of which 160 fat quarters now encumber the deck. At an average of 40 lbs. a quarter, this amounted to 6400 lbs. or *about three tons of meat;* and the yacht being hung round with it in every possible place, it gives her the appearance of a butcher's shop, full of prize oxen, at Christmas.

Early in the morning of the 5th of September we got the anchor up, and bade adieu, with profound regret and heartfelt reluctance, to the gloomy fiords and enchanting ice-floes of Spitzbergen. As those desolate shores faded from our view, I repeated to myself the sublime lines of Longfellow,*

* Discoverer of the North Cape.

"There we hunted the walrus, the narwhal and the seal.
Aha! 'twas a noble game:
And like the lightning's flame
Flew our harpoons of steel."

As we sailed down the west coast we had much calm, and the weather was actually milder than we had had it all the summer. There is evidently an enormous difference of climate between this part of Spitzbergen and the east coast—caused, no doubt, by the great extent of glacier and the vast fields of floating ice in the more immediate vicinity of the latter, as well as by the presence of the fag-end of the Gulf Stream, before alluded to, on *this* coast.

It begins to get a little darkish now from ten till two in the night. One could not have seen to shoot a seal at 10 30 on the 6th. We lighted the cabin and binnacle lamps for the first time to-night at 10 o'clock; and so rapid is the decline of the sun in those latitudes when he once commences to go below the horizon, that on the 7th we had to light them two hours earlier, although we have not made much southing since yesterday.

We had light winds and mild weather all the way across, and only cast anchor in Hammerfest harbor at dusk on the evening of the 11th.

To our great surprise and annoyance, we found that the "Anna Louisa" had only made her number twelve hours before us.

We found a great accumulation of letters and newspapers, and read nearly all night.

On the 12th we got the sloop unloaded and sold the cargo. Owing to the badness of the casks with which we had been provided, a great deal of our blubber was damaged and lost. The price was also very low—as seems always to be the case somehow or other *whenever one has any thing to sell*—but still we realized a sum which went a long way toward paying our expenses; in addition to which we kept the young bears, the six bearskins, and all the ivory.

The 13th and 14th were occupied in getting a stout cage, lined with old iron hoops, made for the bears, settling accounts with our agents, paying off the crew of the sloop, and delivering that sluggish and odoriferous little tub over to her owners.

The crew of the sloop seemed sorry to part with us, and the regret was mutual, for, with one exception, I never met with a more hard-working, docile, uncomplaining, and good-humored lot of fellows than skyppar and crew proved themselves to be.

Although their wages were fully equal in amount to what they would have received on the usual principle of getting for themselves one third of the cargo, we gave the skyppar a handsome additional gratuity, and each of the men (with the exception of the individual above alluded to) a small one. We also told them to divide between them all the bread and other provisions which were left over, but the latter gift unfortunately proved a very "bone of contention," and gave rise to a furious dispute among them. The men who had houses and families wished a division of the actual victuals (the "*ipsa corpora*," as the Rev. Mr. —— calls the oatmeal which I have annually the honor of paying him for), whereas the men who lived *en garçon* contended that the obvious intentions of the munificent donors had been that the provisions should be sold *en masse*, and the proceeds then divided with a view to their immediate convertibility into brandy. As we declined to give any decision on this delicate point, the last we heard of it was, that they had called in the intervention of the merchants who had acted as our agents, and I think it not improbable that these gentlemen settled the matter somewhat after the manner in which the oyster of the fable was partitioned by the referee in that notable case.

We sailed on the 15th, and as we had experienced northeast winds all the way from Leith to Hammerfest, it was quite to be expected in the nature of things that we should have southwest ones all the way back. *We did so*, and in addition we had an awful hustling from the equinoctial gales in the end of the month. We religiously avoided Lerwick this time, for fear the famishing population might storm the yacht to get possession of our cargo of venison, and at last cast anchor in Leith Roads on Sunday, the 2d of October.

For the first few days the climate of Scotland seemed oppressively hot, and I could sympathize with the feelings of the young bears, who appeared ready to melt into oil at this unwonted temperature.

With the view of disposing of these interesting animals, I entered into correspondence with nearly every wild-beast-keeper and secretary of Zoological Gardens in the United Kingdom, but, *as usual*, the "British market was quite overstocked." There was a "glut" of bears, in fact. It then occurred to me that I could not put them to better account than by turning them out in a large wood at home, and inviting my friends and neighbors to enjoy the Scandinavian diversion of a "*skall;*" but the probable difficulty of obtaining *beaters* occurred to me as *one* objection, and the possibility of being brought in for heavy *game damages* as *another;* so eventually I disposed of them to M. le Directeur of the Jardin des Plantes in Paris, and I wish his imperial majesty joy of his purchase. I had the satisfaction of seeing them in that establishment some months later, considerably grown, but their naturally amiable dispositions not improved by their being confined in one of the warm, dry dens used for the tropical Carnivora.

They did *not*, like the lion in the story, recognize and welcome their old shipmate with transports of joy.

In conclusion, I beg to direct attention to the following fac-simile of an engraving executed by Lord David Kennedy on one of the cabin-beams of the

"Anna Louisa," as it contains a concise summary of our game-list.

LORD DAVID KENNEDY
and JAMES LAMONT

HIRED this SLOOP

ANNA LOUISA, not A 1,

In the Summer of the Year 1859,

AND KILLED in SPITZBERGEN

46 WALRUSES,
88 SEALS,
8 POLAR BEARS,
1 WHITE WHALE,
61 REINDEER.

TOTAL, 204 HEAD.

N.B.—In addition to the above, we sunk and lost about 20 Walruses and 40 Seals.

APPENDIX.

APPENDIX.

A LIST OF THE SPECIMENS OF ROCKS, FOSSILS, ANIMALS, &c., SENT TO THE GEOLOGICAL SOCIETY AND NOW IN THEIR MUSEUM.

From Black Point.—Grayish, fine-grained, laminated sandstone, sometimes micaceous.

Brownish, fine-grained, micaceous, shaly sandstone, weathering white.

Pebbles of hard coal.

Brownish-gray limestone, with *Nucula*, *Aviculopecten*, and *Spirifer*.

Gray limestone with calcareous veins. With a trace of calamite?

Fossil wood with attached coaly matter.

From Thousand Islands.—More or less rounded fragments of

Compact red syenitic rock.

Gray compact silicious limestone with corals, *Aviculopecten*, *Streptorhynchus*, &c.

Brownish argillaceous rock.

Yellowish fossiliferous silicious limestone.

White fossiliferous limestone.

Black flint with chalcedonic vein.

White flint or chert.

Purplish semitransparent quartz rock.

Greenstone.

Thin-bedded, gray, compact, silicio-argillaceous rock, with a large *Aviculopecten*.

Hard compact sandstone.

Red, highly silicious limestone.

Greenstone, coarse-grained, with weathered face.

From Ryk-Yse Islands.—Rounded fragments of gray compact limestone with *Fenestellæ* and corals.

From Ice Sound.—Fine-grained, compact, dark gray sandstone, weathering ferruginous.

Ferruginous nodules (exfoliating) of the size of cannon balls.

From Island, Bell Sound.—Weathered fragment of argillo-silicious dark gray rock, with *Fenestella* and corals.

Hard reddish ferruginous rock, with pebbles of Lydian stone.

Fossils, from 200 feet above the sea, and 350 yards inland. (See Mr. Salter's Appendix.)

Brownish-gray, micaceous, compact, fine-grained sandstone pebbles, with trace of the cast of an *Aviculopecten?*

From Bell Sound.—Fossils from 400 feet above the sea level. (See Mr. Salter's Appendix.)

From Moraine in Deeva Bay.—Brown claystone, weathering reddish-purple.

Different Localities.

Ferruginous nodule, small.

Hard ferruginous sandstone with small ferruginous nodule.

Silicious conglomerate.

Boulder of conglomerate, or coarse pebbly grit; pebbles of white and dark gray quartz and Lydian stone, cement calcareous.

White quartz rock.

Stem-like piece of brownish fine-grained sandstone (? cast of a ripple-mark).

Light-gray friable sandstone.

Dark-gray mudstone (calcareo-argillaceous) with impression of shell.

Water-worn fragment of tortuously laminated calcareous slate.

Pebble of gray argillaceous limestone with calc-spar vein.

Bouldered piece of gray silicious limestone with *Productus* and corals.

Gray silicious limestone with *Orthis* and *Productus*, with weathered surface.

White crystalline limestone with *Spirifer cristatus* and corals, having a weathered surface.

White silicious limestone with corals, *Encrinites*, and shells.

Black silicious limestone with calcareous veins.

Weathered fragment of white encrinital chert with coals, *Bryozoa* (?), and *Productus*.

Black flint with whitish mottlings, splinters.

Red silicious limestone with a rounded, weathered surface.

Probably from the Thousand Islands.

(Islands to the south-east ?) Weathered fragment of white limestone with *Productus*, *Spirifer alatus*, and a large foliaceous coral (*Stenopora*).

RECENT SHELLS (determined by S. P. WOODWARD, Esq., F.G.S.).

1. From the Thousand Isles.
   Buccinum undatum, var. (*cyaneum* ? ?).

2. From Bell Sound, at about high-water mark.
   Fusus despectus, L., var. (=*F. borealis*, Philippi).
   Buccinum glaciale, L. (=*B. angulosum*=*B. polare*, Beck).
   Margarita undulata (= *Grœnlandica*) inside a *Buccinum*.
   Buccinum scalariforme ?
   Balanus crenatus, var. *Scoticus*, probably.
   Fusus Kroyeri, Möller.

Cardium Islandicum (=*ciliatum*).
Cardium Grœnlandicum (broken).
—— —— (very fine).
Saxicava arctica.
Mya Uddevallensis (*truncata*, var.).
Astarte borealis, Chemn., var. (=*semisulcata*, Leach; =*lactea*, Broderip).
Mya truncata, var. *Uddevallensis.*
Pecten Islandicus.
Nullipore, with *Saxicava.*

3. From Bell Sound, at about 1½ to 2 miles inland, and 400 or 500 feet above the sea level.
Buccinum glaciale (1½ to 2 miles inland, 400 and 500 feet high).

4. From the Moraine of a glacier in Deeva Bay.
Astarte borealis (var. *semisulcata*).
—— *compressa*, Mont., var. *striata.*
Mya truncata, var. *Uddevallensis.*

Bones.

1. Fragment of vertebra of Whale, rotten. Bell Sound. Half a mile from the sea. 100 feet above the sea.
2. Fragment of bone. Half a mile from the sea at Bell Sound. 100 feet above the sea.
3. Cranium of a small *Delphinopterus leucas* (White Whale or Beluga). Bell Sound. 300 yards from the sea. 80 feet above the sea.
4. Anterior rib of a Whale. Bell Sound. 500 yards from the sea. 80 feet high.
5. Small lumbar vertebra of Beluga (?) Bell Sound. Nearly buried at 70 feet above high-tide mark.
6. Fragment of bone of Whale. Bell Sound. Buried in bank 50 feet above the sea.

7. Half a caudal vertebra of Whale. *Balæna mysticetus* (?) Bell Sound. A little above high-water mark.
8. Caudal vertebra of Whale. Found among the boulders at high-water mark. Colored ferruginous.
9. Small cervical vertebra of Beluga?
10. Tibia and fibula of hind left leg of a Walrus.
11. Large caudal vertebra of Whale.
12. Part of lower jaw of Whale. Walter Thymen's Straits. Half a mile from the sea, and 40 feet above sea level.

Quarterly Journal of the Geological Society.

Description of the GRAVELS *from* SPITZBERGEN. By J. PRESTWICH, Esq., F.G.S.

1. Gravel from Bell Sound, 60 feet above high-water mark. Gray gravel of small subangular fragments of dark-gray argillaceous and quartzose slaty rocks, some portions calcareous, and a few fragments of gray sandstone, mixed with a small proportion of earth. None of the fragments are above two ounces in weight, the bulk being of small size (seventy to the ounce). Among these subangular fragments there are, however, a few small round pebbles of a dark-gray limestone, and a few perfectly angular fragments of slate.

There are no shells, nor any characters on any of the fragments in the gravel to indicate a beach-origin. The mass, in fact, looks much more like the smaller fragments of a moraine. None of the fragments, however, are scratched or striated.

2. Gravel from Bell Sound, 20 feet above high-water. Dark-colored grit, clean and uniform in texture, consisting of small subangular fragments of a black hornblende slate (like that of No. 4) about the size of cress-seed, with a very few flattish pebbles of the size of peas, and still fewer rounded pebbles of the size of marbles. There are no fragments of shells.

3. Gravel from an island in Bell Sound, a little above high-water. Small grayish-green gravel of flat angular fragments of greenish mica slate, with a few pieces of quartz. None of

the fragments are an ounce in weight. The bulk consists of pieces of about thirty to the ounce. No matrix of any sort. No fragments of shells. This gravel has the appearance of rock débris *in situ*.

4. Gravel from Bell Sound, halfway between high and low water. Ordinary clean and well-worn small beach-shingle, the smaller fragments being more or less subangular, and the larger ones more or less rounded: no fragments above three quarters of an ounce in weight; and the bulk 117 to the ounce. It is composed mostly of compact black hornblende slate (like that of No. 2), compact gray sandstone, and some gray limestone and a very little quartz. There are no shells nor scratched pebbles. It is much like the shingle of parts of our own coast.

5. Gravel from Bell Sound, low-water anchorage. Subangular small fragments of micaceous slates, with a few flat angular fragments of limestone. Not one well-rounded pebble; few even of the fragments are much worn. There are no shells. This looks much like the small débris in an old slate quarry.

Note on the Fossils *from* Spitzbergen. By J. W. Salter, Esq., F.G.S.

The specimens of fossils brought by Mr. Lamont are chiefly from three localities, viz.:

1. Bell Sound (at 400 feet above the sea level), western side of the island;

2. Island in Bell Sound (at 200 feet above the sea, and 350 yards from the shore); and,

3. Black Point, near the S.E. angle of Spitzbergen, close to which are the Thousand Isles.

From Bell Sound only a few species were collected; and these are the same as those from the small island in the same Sound. One is a large *Productus*, which I can not identify completely with any British species. It may be a large variety of one of our common shells, *P. semireticulatus*, or even a form of *P. Costatus*. In any case it is of a Carboniferous type.

The specimens from the island in Bell Sound are much more numerous; and in a gray limestone we have,

1. *Athyris* or *Spirifer*, a large smooth species, nearly 3 inches across, without any definite hinge-line, and with very strong ventral muscular impressions. The shell is much depressed.

2. *Productus costatus*, Sowerby, very large, and deeply bilobed. Abundant.

3. *Productus*, the large striate species above mentioned.

4. *P. Humboldtii*, D'Orbigny, two or three specimens.

5. *P. mammatus*, Keyserling (?), or an allied species, without large scattering spines. This species occurs in Arctic America, having been brought by Captain Belcher from the point opposite Exmouth Island. It is the *P. Leplayii* of De Koninck's paper on the Fossils from Spitzbergen, but not, I think, of De Verneuil, who described that species in "Russia in Europe."

Von Buch quotes the *Productus giganteus* from the South Cape and from Bell Sound: this is not noticed at all in Prof. Koninck's list (1849, *op. cit.*, p. 633).

6. *Camarophoria*, a large species, not unlike in shape to the *Rhynchonella acuminata* of the Carboniferous limestone, but ribbed throughout.

7. *Spirifer Keilhavii*, Von Buch. Several specimens. This, more than any other shell, tends to connect the Spitzbergen formation with surrounding districts. *Sp. Keilhavii* was described in the Berlin Trans. for May, 1846. The specimens were brought home by Keilhau from the rocks of Bear Island, in 74° 30′ N. lat., half way between Norway and Spitzbergen. In the same paper Von Buch notices that the locality of Bell Sound had been visited by French naturalists (M. Robert and the Scientific Commission which explored these seas in 1839), and that the same *Producti* and *Spirifer* (*S. Keilhavii*) were

found there which occurred at Bear Island. And, inasmuch as the *Producti* are the common British species *P. giganteus* and *P. Cora*, there can be no doubt whatever of the formation to which *Spirifer Keilhavii* belongs. Count Keyserling described a variety of it from Petschora Land under another name; and in the Appendix to Belcher's "Last of the Arctic Voyages" I have figured and described this shell from the Carboniferous rocks of North Albert Land—Captain Belcher's farthest point. Numerous *Producti* occurred with it, two of which, if not more, are identical with the Spitzbergen species. I notice this more particularly, because in two communications to the Royal Academy of Brussels (Bulletin, vols. xiii. and xiv.) Prof. de Koninck has described the Bell Sound fossils as Permian, and not Carboniferous species, and has given figures of several of them. In a short résumé of the Arctic Geology read by myself to the British Association, 1855, I have used this fact as illustrative of the regularity of the great Arctic basin of Palæozoic rocks (Trans. Sect., p. 211).

One species only which appears to me of Permian date occurs in a loose block (without definite locality), and will be presently noticed. It would be somewhat remarkable if all the specimens brought home by M. Robert should prove to be Permian, while those from the same locality before us are mostly of Carboniferous type. The larger and more conspicuous shells do not seem to have been met with by M. Robert in his voyage.

8. *Fenestella*, two species, one with very large meshes.

9. Sponges (?); large, stem-like and cake-like in shape.

Specimens without definite localities:

10. *Spirifer cristatus*, Schloth. *S. octoplicatus* of the mountain limestone is now regarded as the same species.

11. *Streptorhynchus crenistria*, or an allied form.

12. *Zaphrentis Ovibos*, Salter (?). Probably an Arctic species.

13. *Stenopora*; a large branched species, like *S. Tasmaniensis* of Lonsdale. This occurs at Bell Sound also.

14. *Syringopora*, large fragments.

15. A new genus, in all probability of the *Fenestellidæ*, consisting of thick stems branching regularly from opposite sides, the smaller branches also opposite, and coalescing also with their neighbors so as to form a quadrangular net-work. But for this coalescence it might be a gigantic *Thamniscus* or *Ichthyorhachis*. As the poriferous face is not seen, it is better not to give a new generic name.

From Black Point, in shaly beds, which seem to be associated with the coal, slabs were obtained with numerous shells and some fragments of plants.

16. *Nucula*, abundant; and among these is a small

17. *Aviculopecten*, and a *Spirifer* with broad ribs.

18. *Aviculopecten*. A large species (looking like the *A. papyraceus* of our own coal-shales magnified), found in the gravel among the Thousand Isles; it probably came from these beds.

A weathered block of white limestone, probably from the islands on the southeastern side of Spitzbergen,* contains the only truly Permian species which I have seen among these specimens, viz.,

19. *Spirifer alatus*, Schloth., a common fossil of the Zechstein.

20. *Productus*, a small species. (*P. Horridus* of De Koninck's list, but apparently too deeply lobed.)

21. *Stenopora*, a large foliaceous flattened species.

Spirifer octoplicatus (*cristatus*), above mentioned, also oc-

* With regard to this specimen, I stated, in reply to an inquiry on the subject, "The loose block of white limestone to which you refer as 'having a Permian aspect' was, if I mistake not, picked up on one of the islands to the S.E. of Edge's Land. It is unlike any rock I saw *in situ*; and, as it is evidently a traveled block, I think it not improbable that it does not belong to Spitzbergen at all, but may have been transported by the drift-ice from Commander Gillies's Land, or some other unknown country to the northeast."—April 21, 1860.—J. L.

curs in similar whitish limestone. These may possibly have all come from the locality whence M. Robert's original specimens were found; but it would appear that they are not by any means the prevailing fossils of the island.

The general aspect of the fossils is unquestionably carboniferous, and some of the species have a wide diffusion. *Productus costatus* ranges from India to the Mississippi, and *P. semireticulatus* (which I think is only a variety of the same species) has even a wider range.* *P. Humboldtii* is found in Russia and South America. Our *P. mammatus?* is probably distinct from the Russian species, but it is, at all events, the same as one in Captain Belcher's collection.†

The size of the fossils, both of the shells and Bryozoa, is remarkable, and, taken in conjunction with the presence of large land-plants in the coal, would seem to indicate a great decrease of temperature in the Arctic region since the Carboniferous period. The shells are larger, too, than the corresponding species in our own mountain limestone.‡

* To Australia (M'Coy).

† It is closely and finely striate, and has spines along the hinge-line only.

‡ Quarterly Journal of the Geological Society.

THE END.

STANDARD LIBRARY WORKS

PUBLISHED BY

HARPER & BROTHERS, NEW YORK.

☞ Harper & Brothers will send either of the following Works by Mail, postage prepaid (for any distance in the United States under 3000 miles), on receipt of the Money.

☞ Harper & Brothers' New Descriptive Catalogue of their Publications may be obtained gratuitously on application to the Publishers personally, or by letter inclosing Six Cents in Postage Stamps.

Abbott's History of the French Revolution. With 100 Engravings. 8vo, Muslin, $2 50; Half Calf, $3 50.

Abbott's History of Napoleon Bonaparte. With Maps, Wood-cuts, and Portraits on Steel. 2 vols. 8vo, Muslin, $5 00; Sheep, $5 75; Half Calf, $7 00; Turkey Morocco, $10 00.

Abbott's Napoleon at St. Helena. Interesting Anecdotes and Remarkable Conversations of the Emperor during the Five and a Half Years of his Captivity. From the Memorials of Las Casas, O'Meara, Montholon, Antommarchi, &c. With Illustrations. 8vo, Muslin, $2 50; Sheep, $2 87½; Half Calf, $3 50.

Addison's Complete Works, embracing the whole of the "Spectator." Complete in 3 vols. 8vo, Sheep extra, $4 50; Half Calf, $6 75.

Alford's Greek Testament. The Greek Testament: with a Critically Revised Text; a Digest of Various Readings; Marginal References to Verbal and Idiomatic Usage; Prolegomena; and a Critical and Exegetical Commentary. For the use of Theological Students and Ministers. By Henry Alford, B.D., Minister of Quebec Chapel, London, and late Fellow of Trinity College, Cambridge. Vol. I., containing the Four Gospels. 944 pages, 8vo, Muslin, $5 00; Sheep extra, $5 50; Half Calf extra, $6 00.

Alison's History of Europe, complete. First Series.—From the Commencement of the French Revolution, in 1789, to the Restoration of the Bourbons, in 1815. In addition to the Notes on Chapter LXXVI., which correct the Errors of the Original Work concerning the United States, a copious Analytical Index has been appended to this American Edition. 4 vols. 8vo, Muslin, $6 00; Sheep extra, $7 00; Half Calf, $10 00.

Second Series.—From the Fall of Napoleon, in 1815, to the Accession of Louis Napoleon, in 1852. With a copious Analytical Index. 4 vols. 8vo, Muslin, $6 00; Sheep extra, $7 00; Half Calf, $10 00.

Alison's Military Life of John, Duke of Marlborough. With Maps. 12mo, Muslin, $1 50; Half Calf, $2 35.

Atkinson's Oriental and Western Siberia. Map and numerous Illustrations from Drawings by the Author. 8vo, Muslin, $3 00; Half Calf, $4 00.

Atkinson's Travels in the Regions of the Upper and Lower Amoor and the Russian Acquisitions on the Confines of India and China. With Adventures among the Mountain Kirghis; and the Manjours, Manyargs, Toungouz, Touzemtz, Goldi, and Gelyaks; the Hunting and Pastoral Tribes. With a Map and numerous Illustrations. 8vo, Muslin, $2 50; Half Calf, $3 50.

Barth's Travels and Discoveries in North and Central Africa. Profusely and elegantly Illustrated. The only complete American Edition. 3 vols. 8vo, Muslin, $7 50; Half Calf, $10 50.

Bancroft's Literary and Historical Miscellanies. 8vo, Muslin, $2 00; Half Calf, $3 00.

Barnes's Notes on the New Testament. For Bible Classes and Sunday-Schools. Maps and Engravings. 11 vols. 12mo, Muslin, 75 cents per volume; Half Calf, $17 60 per set. The Vols. sold separately.

Blackstone's Commentaries on the Laws of England. With copious Notes, adapting the Work to the American Student. By John L. Wendell, late State Reporter of New York. 4 vols. 8vo, Law Sheep, $7 00.

Boswell's Life of Dr. Johnson. Portrait of Boswell. 2 vols. 8vo, Sheep extra, $3 00; Half Calf, $4 50.

Brodhead's History of the State of New York. First Period, 1609–1664. 8vo, Muslin, $3 00; Half Calf, $4 00.

Bulwer's Novels. Harper's Library Edition, in handsome 12mo, $1 00 per vol. *Now Ready:* The Caxtons, 1 vol.—"My Novel," 2 vols. Half Calf, $1 85 per vol.

Bunting's (Rev. Dr. Jabez) Life. With Notices of Contemporary Persons and Events. By his Son, Thomas Percival Bunting. Vol. I., with a Portrait. 12mo, Muslin, $1 00.

Burke's Complete Works. With a Memoir. Portrait. 3 vols. 8vo, Sheep extra, $4 50; Half Calf, $6 75.

Burns's Life and Works. Edited by Robert Chambers. 4 vols. 12mo, Muslin, $3 00; Half Calf, $6 40.

Burr's Memoirs, with Miscellaneous Correspondence. By M. L. Davis. Portraits. 8vo, Muslin, $3 00; Half Calf, $5 00.

Burr's Private Journal, during his Residence in Europe; with Selections from his Correspondence. By M. L. Davis. 2 vols. 8vo, Muslin, $4 50; Half Calf, $6 50.

Burton's Lake Regions of Central Africa. A Picture of Exploration. By Richard F. Burton, Capt. H.M.I. Army. With Maps and Engravings on Wood. 8vo, Muslin, $3 00; Half Calf, $4 00.

Carlyle's History of Frederick the Great. 4 vols. 12mo, Muslin, $1 25 each; Half Calf, $2 10 each. Vols. I. and II., with Portraits and Maps, now ready.

Carlyle's French Revolution. 2 vols. 12mo, Muslin, $2 00; Half Calf, $3 70.

Carlyle's Oliver Cromwell. 2 vols. 12mo, Muslin, $2 00; Half Calf, $3 70.

Carlyle's Past and Present, Chartism, and Sartor Resartus. 12mo, Muslin, $1 00; Half Calf, $1 85.

Chalmers's Life and Writings. 4 vols. 12mo, Muslin, $1 00 per vol.; Half Calf, $7 40 per set.

Chalmers's Posthumous Works. Edited by his Son-in-law, Rev. WILLIAM HANNA, LL.D. Complete in 9 vols. 12mo, Muslin, $1 00 each; Sheep extra, $1 12½ each; Half Calf, $16 65 per set. Comprising DAILY SCRIPTURE READINGS, 3 vols.; SABBATH SCRIPTURE READINGS, 2 vols.; SERMONS, from 1798 to 1847, 1 vol.; INSTITUTES OF THEOLOGY, 2 vols.; PRELECTIONS ON BUTLER'S ANALOGY, PALEY'S EVIDENCES OF CHRISTIANITY, and HILL'S LECTURES ON DIVINITY, with two Introductory Lectures and Four Addresses, delivered in the New College, Edinburgh, 1 vol. The vols. sold separately.

Chalmers's Correspondence. 1 vol. 12mo, Muslin, $1 00; Half Calf, $1 85.

Claiborne's Life and Correspondence of John A. Quitman, Major-General U.S.A., and Governor of the State of Mississippi. Portrait. 2 vols. 12mo, Muslin, $3 00.

Coleridge's Complete Works. With an Introductory Essay upon his Philosophical and Theological Opinions. Edited by Professor SHEDD. Complete in 7 vols. Portrait. Small 8vo, Muslin, $7 00; Half Calf, $13 00. The vols. sold separately.

VOL. I. Aids to Reflection.—Statesman's Manual. II. The Friend. III. Biographia Literaria. IV. Lectures on Shakspeare and Other Dramatists. V. Literary Remains. VI. Second Lay Sermon and Table-Talk. VII. Poetical and Dramatic Works.

Crabb's English Synonyms. 8vo, Sheep extra, $2 00.

Creasy's Fifteen Decisive Battles of the World: from Marathon to Waterloo. 12mo, Muslin, $1 00; Half Calf, $1 85.

Curran and his Contemporaries. By CHARLES PHILLIPS. 12mo, Muslin, 87½ cents; Half Calf, $1 82.

Geo. Wm. Curtis's Works:

Trumps. Illustrated by HOPPIN. 12mo, Muslin.

The Potiphar Papers. Illustrated from Drawings by DARLEY. 12mo, Muslin, $1 00; Half Calf, $1 85.

Prue and I. 12mo, Muslin, $1 00; Half Calf, $1 85.

Lotus-Eating. A Summer-Book. Beautifully Illustrated from Designs by KENSETT. 12mo, Muslin, 75 cents; Half Calf, $1 60.

The Howadji in Syria. 12mo, Muslin, $1 00; Half Calf, $1 85.

Nile Notes of a Howadji. 12mo, Muslin, $1 00; Half Calf, $1 85.

Davis's Carthage and her Remains: being an Account of the Excavations and Researches on the site of the Phœnician Metropolis in Africa and other adjacent Places. Conducted under the Auspices of Her Majesty's Government. By Dr. N. DAVIS, F.R.G.S., &c. With Illustrations. 8vo, Muslin.

De Tocqueville's Old Regime and the French Revolution. Translated by JOHN BONNER. 12mo, Muslin, $1 00; Half Calf, $1 85.

D'Israeli's Amenities of Literature. 2 vols. 12mo, Muslin, $1 50; Half Calf, $3 20.

Dante's Inferno. A Literal Prose Translation. By JOHN A. CARLYLE, M.D. 12mo, Muslin, $1 00; Half Calf, $1 85.

Draper's Human Physiology, Statical and Dynamical; or, The Conditions and Course of the Life of Man. Illustrated by nearly 300 fine Wood-cuts from Photographs. New Edition. 8vo, 650 pages, Muslin, $4 00; Sheep, $4 25; Half Calf, $5 00.

Dryden's Complete Works. With Life, by MITFORD. 2 vols. 8vo, Sheep extra, $3 00; Half Calf, $4 50.

Dwight's Theology, in a Series of Sermons. With Memoir of the Author. Portrait. 4 vols. 8vo, Muslin, $6 00; Sheep extra, $6 50; Half Calf, $10 00.

Miss Edgeworth's Tales and Novels. Engravings. 10 vols. 12mo, Muslin, $7 50; Half Calf, $16 00. The vols. sold separately in Muslin.

Ellis's Three Visits to Madagascar, during the Years 1853–1854–1856. Including a Journey to the Capital, with Notices of the Natural History of the Country and the Present Civilization of the People. Map and Wood-cuts from Photographs. Complete and unabridged. 8vo, Muslin, $2 50.

Forster's Celebrated British Statesmen. Portraits. 8vo, Sheep extra, $1 50; Half Calf, $2 25.

Fowler's English Language, in its Elements and Forms. With a History of its Origin and Development, and a full Grammar. New and Revised Edition. 8vo, Muslin, $1 50; Sheep extra, $1 75.

Franklin's Life, Illustrated. With numerous exquisite Designs, by JOHN G. CHAPMAN. 8vo, Muslin, $2 00; Sheep, $2 25; Half Calf, $3 00.

Gibbon's History of the Decline and Fall of the Roman Empire. With Notes, by Rev. H. H. MILMAN and M. GUIZOT. Maps and Engravings, complete Index and Portrait of the Author. 6 vols. 12mo (uniform with Hume and Macaulay), Muslin, $3 75; Sheep extra, $4 50; Half Calf, $9 00.

Gieseler's Church History. Translated. A New American Edition, Revised and Edited by Rev. HENRY B. SMITH, D.D. Vols. I., II., and III. 8vo, Sheep, $6 75; Half Calf, $9 00.

Godwin's History of France. From the Earliest Times to the French Revolution of 1789. Vol. I. (Ancient Gaul.) 8vo, Muslin, $2 00.

Goodrich's Select British Eloquence; embracing the best Speeches entire of the most eminent Orators of Great Britain for the last two Centuries; with Sketches of their Lives, an Estimate of their Genius, and Notes Critical and Explanatory. 8vo, Muslin, $3 50; Sheep extra, $3 75; Half Calf, $4 50.

Grote's History of Greece. 12 vols. 12mo, Muslin, $9 00; Half Calf, $19 20 per Set.

Hale's (Mrs.) Woman's Record; or, Biographical Sketches of all Distinguished Women, from the Creation to the Present Time. With Selections from Female Writers of each Era. More than 200 Portraits, engraved by LOSSING. 8vo, Muslin, $3 50.

Hallam's Historical Works. 4 vols. 8vo, Sheep extra, $7 00; Half Calf, $10 00.

Hall's (Rev. Robert) Complete Works. Memoir by Dr. GREGORY, and Observations on his Character as a Preacher, by Rev. JOHN FOSTER. Portrait. 4 vols. 12mo, Sheep extra, $6 00; Half Calf, $9 00.

Sir William Hamilton's Discussions on Philosophy, Literature, and University Reform. Chiefly from the Edinburgh Review. Corrected, Vindicated, Enlarged, in Notes and Appendices. 8vo, Muslin, $1 50; Half Calf, $2 50.

Homans's Cyclopædia of Commerce and Commercial Navigation. Royal 8vo, 2000 pages, Muslin, 1 vol., $6 00; Sheep, 1 vol., $6 75; Half Calf, 1 vol., $8 00; Sheep, 2 vols., $8 00; Law Sheep, 2 vols., $8 00; Half Calf, 2 vols., $8 75.

Harper's New Classical Library. Literal Translations of Greek and Latin Authors. 12mo, Muslin, 75 cents per vol.; Half Calf, $1 60 per vol. Comprising CÆSAR, VIRGIL, SALLUST, HORACE, CICERO'S ORATIONS, CICERO'S OFFICES, &c., CICERO ON ORATORY AND ORATORS, TACITUS, 2 vols., TERENCE, JUVENAL, XENOPHON, HOMER'S ILIAD, HOMER'S ODYSSEY, HERODOTUS, DEMOSTHENES, 2 vols., THUCYDIDES, ÆSCHYLUS, SOPHOCLES, EURIPIDES, 2 vols.

Head's Daily Walk with Wise Men; or, Religious Exercises for Every Day in the Year. Selected, Arranged, and specially adapted, by Rev. NELSON HEAD. Large 12mo, Muslin. (*Nearly Ready.*)

Helps's Spanish Conquest in America, and its Relation to the History of Slavery and to the Government of the Colonies. 3 vols. 12mo, Muslin, $3 00; Half Calf, $5 50.

Hildreth's History of the United States. FIRST SERIES.—From the First Settlement of the Country to the Adoption of the Federal Constitution. 3 vols. 8vo, Muslin, $6 00; Sheep extra, $6 75; Half Calf, $9 00.

SECOND SERIES. —From the Adoption of the Federal Constitution to the End of the Sixteenth Congress. 3 vols. 8vo, Muslin, $6 00; Sheep extra, $6 75; Half Calf, $9 00.

Humboldt's Cosmos. 6 vols. 12mo, Muslin, $4 25; Half Calf, $8 50.

Hume's History of England. 5 vols. 12mo, Muslin, $3 75; Sheep, $4 50; Half Calf, $9 00. (Uniform with Macaulay and Gibbon.)

Jay's Complete Works. 3 vols. 8vo, Sheep extra, $4 50; Half Calf, $6 75.

Johnson's Complete Works. Portrait. 2 vols. 8vo, Sheep extra, $3 00; Half Calf, $4 50.

Lamartine's History of the Girondists; or, Personal Memoirs of the Patriots of the French Revolution. From unpublished Sources. 3 vols. 12mo, Muslin, $2 10; Half Calf, $4 65.

Lamartine's Memoirs of Celebrated Characters. 3 vols. 12mo, Muslin, $2 63; Half Calf, $5 20.

Lamb's Works. Comprising his Letters, Poems, Essays of Elia, Essays upon Shakspeare, Hogarth, &c., and a Sketch of his Life, with the Final Memorials, by T. NOON TALFOURD. Portrait. 2 vols. 12mo, Muslin, $2 00; Half Calf, $3 70.

Layard's Popular Account of the Discoveries at Nineveh. Abridged. With numerous Wood Engravings. 12mo, Muslin, 75 cents; Half Calf, $1 60.

Layard's Fresh Discoveries in Nineveh and Babylon; with Travels in Armenia, Kurdistan, and the Desert: being the Result of a Second Expedition, undertaken for the Trustees of the British Museum. With all of the Maps and Engravings in the English Edition. 8vo, Muslin, $2 25; Half Calf, $3 25.

Livingstone's Missionary Travels and Researches in South Africa. Maps by ARROWSMITH, a Portrait on Steel, and numerous Illustrations. Only complete American edition. With elaborate Index. 8vo, Muslin, $3 00; Half Calf, $4 00.

Macaulay's History of England, from the Accession of James II. With an original Portrait of the Author. A HANDSOME OCTAVO LIBRARY EDITION, on superfine Paper, Muslin, $1 50 a volume; Half Calf, $2 50.—A POPULAR DUODECIMO EDITION. With Portrait and Index. Printed on fine Paper, Muslin, 62½ cents; Half Calf, $1 50.—A CHEAP OCTAVO EDITION. Paper Covers, 25 cents a volume.—A CHEAP OCTAVO EDITION. The four volumes neatly bound in two volumes, Muslin, 62½ cents a volume. The volumes of any of the above editions sold separately.

Maury's Physical Geography of the Sea. Wood-cuts and Charts. New Edition, greatly Enlarged and Improved. 8vo, Muslin, $1 50; Half Calf, $2 50.

Mill's Logic. 8vo, Muslin, $1 50.

Mills's Literature and Literary Men of Great Britain and Ireland. 2 vols. 8vo, Muslin, $3 50; Half Calf, $5 50.

Hannah More's Complete Works. Engravings. 8vo, Sheep extra, $2 50; Half Calf, $3 25. Muslin, 2 vols., $2 75; Half Calf, $4 25. The same Work, printed from large type, 7 vols. 12mo, Muslin, $5 25; Half Calf, $11 20.

Hannah More's Life and Correspondence. By W. ROBERTS. 2 vols. 12mo, Muslin, $1 50; Half Calf, $3 20.

Mosheim's Ecclesiastical History. Ancient and Modern. 2 vols. 8vo, Sheep extra, $3 00; Half Calf, $4 50.

Motley's Rise of the Dutch Republic. A History. 3 vols. 8vo, Muslin, $6 00; Sheep, $6 75; Half Calf, $9 00.

Motley's History of the United Netherlands. 2 vols. 8vo, Muslin, $4 00.

Neale's History of the Puritans. 2 vols. 8vo, Muslin, $2 75; Sheep extra, $3 00; Half Calf, $4 50.

Neander's Life of Christ. Translated by Professors MCCLINTOCK and BLUMENTHAL. 8vo, Muslin, $2 00; Sheep extra, $2 25; Half Calf, $3 00.

Page's La Plata: The Argentine Confederation and Paraguay. Being a Narrative of the Exploration of the Tributaries of the River La Plata and Adjacent Countries during the Years 1853, '54, '55, and '56, under the orders of the United States Government. With Map and numerous Engravings. 8vo, Muslin, $3 00; Half Calf, $4 00.

Miss Pardoe's Louis XIV. and the Court of France in the Seventeenth Century. Illustrated with numerous Engravings. Portraits, &c. 2 vols. 12mo, Muslin, $3 50; Half Calf, $5 20.

Plutarch's Lives. Portrait. 8vo, Sheep, $1 25. Large type, 4 vols. 12mo, Sheep extra, $3 50; Half Calf, $6 50.

Robertson's Historical Works: Discovery of America. 8vo, Sheep extra, $1 50; Half Calf, $2 25.—Charles V. 8vo, Sheep extra, $1 50; Half Calf, $2 25.—Scotland and Ancient India. 8vo, Sheep extra, $1 50; Half Calf, $2 25.

Prime's Boat Life in Egypt and Nubia. Illustrations. 12mo, Muslin, $1 25; Half Calf, $2 10.

Prime's Tent Life in the Holy Land. Illustrations. 12mo, Muslin, $1 25; Half Calf, $2 10.

Prime's Coins, Medals, and Seals, Ancient and Modern. Illustrated and Described. 8vo, Muslin, $2 50.

Rollin's Ancient History. Numerous Maps and Engravings. In 2 vols. 8vo, Sheep extra, $2 75. 1 vol., Sheep, $2 50.

Russell's History of Modern Europe. Engravings. 3 vols. 8vo, Sheep, $4 50.

Miss Sedgwick's Works. Embracing Memoir of Joseph Curtis. 16mo, Muslin, 50 c.—Married or Single. 2 vols. 12mo, Muslin, $1 75; Half Calf, $3 45.—Letters from Abroad to Kindred at Home. 2 vols. 12mo, Muslin, $1 90; Half Calf, $3 60.—Live and Let Live; or, Domestic Service Illustrated. 18mo, Muslin, 45 c.—Means and Ends; or, Self-training. 18mo, Muslin, 45 c.—A Love-Token for Children. 18mo, Muslin, 45 c.—The Poor Rich Man and the Rich Poor Man. 18mo, Muslin, 45 c.—Stories for Young Persons. 18mo, Muslin, 45 c.—Wilton Harvey, and Other Tales. 18mo, Muslin, 45 cents.—The Linwoods. 2 vols. 12mo, Muslin, $1 50; Half Calf, $3 20.

Saurin's Sermons. Portrait. 2 vols. Sheep extra, $3 00; Half Calf, $4 50.

Shakspeare's Dramatic Works. Engravings. 6 vols. 12mo, Muslin, $4 50; Half Calf, $9 60.

Mrs. Sigourney's Works. Lucy Howard's Journal. 16mo, Muslin, 75 c.—Letters to Mothers. 12mo, Muslin, 75 c.; Muslin, gilt edges, 90 c.—Letters to Young Ladies. 12mo, Muslin, 75 c.; Muslin, gilt edges, 90 c.—Myrtis, and Other Sketchings. 12mo, Muslin, 75 c.; Half Calf, $1 60.—Pocahontas, and Other Poems. Engravings. 12mo, Muslin, 90 c.; Half Calf, $1 75.

Sismondi's Historical View of the Literature of the South of Europe. 2 vols. 12mo, Muslin, $1 80; Half Calf, $3 50.

Smiles's Self-Help. With Illustrations of Character and Conduct. New Edition, Revised and Enlarged, with Portraits on Wood, chiefly by Lossing. 12mo, Muslin, 50 cents.

Sparks's Library of American Biography. 10 vols. 12mo, Muslin, $7 50. The volumes sold separately, at 75 cents each; Half Calf, $16 00 a set.

Squier's Nicaragua: Its People, Scenery, Monuments, Resources, Conditions, and Proposed Canal. Revised Edition. With 100 Maps and Illustrations. 8vo, Muslin, $3 00; Half Calf, $4 00.

Squier's States of Central America: their Geography, Topography, Climate, Population, Resources, Productions, Commerce, Political Organizations, Aborigines, &c., &c. Comprising Chapters on Honduras, San Salvador, Nicaragua, Costa Rica, Guatemala, Belize, the Bay Islands, the Mosquito Shore, and the Honduras Inter-Oceanic Railway. With numerous Original Maps and Illustrations. A New and Enlarged Edition. 8vo, Muslin, $3 00; Half Calf, $4 00.

Stephen's (Sir James) Lectures on the History of France. 8vo, Muslin, $1 75; Half Calf, $2 75.

Stephens's (John L.) Works. Travels in Central America, Chiapas, and Yucatan. With a Map and 88 Engravings. 2 vols. 8vo, Muslin, $5 00; Half Calf, $7 00.

Incidents of Travel in Yucatan. 120 Engravings, from Drawings by F. Catherwood. 2 vols. 8vo, Muslin, $5; Half Calf, $7.

Travels in Greece, Turkey, Russia, and Poland. Engravings. 2 vols. 12mo, Muslin, $1 75; Half Calf, $3 45.

Travels in Egypt, Arabia Petræa, and the Holy Land. Engravings. 2 vols. 12mo, Muslin, $1 75; Half Calf, $3 45.

Strickland's (Miss) Queens of Scotland. Complete in 8 vols. 12mo, Muslin, $1 00 each; Sets in Muslin, $8 00; Half Calf, $14 80.

Taylor's Wesley and Methodism. 12mo, Muslin, 75 cents; Half Calf, $1 60.

Taylor's World of Mind. 12mo, Muslin, $1 00; Half Calf, $1 85.

Thackeray's Works:

The Four Georges. With Illustrations by the Author. 12mo, Muslin, 75 cts.

English Humorists of the Eighteenth Century. Together with his Lecture on "Charity and Humor." 12mo, Muslin, $1 00; Half Calf, $1 85.

The Virginians. A Tale of the Last Century. With Illustrations by the Author. 8vo, Paper, $1 75; Muslin, $2 00; Half Calf, $3 00.

The Newcomes. 8vo, Muslin, $2 00; Half Calf, $3 00.

Vanity Fair. 8vo, Muslin, $1 25; Half Calf, $2 25.

Pendennis. 2 vols. 8vo, Muslin, $2 00; Half Calf, $4 00.

Thirlwall's History of Greece. 2 vols. 8vo, Muslin, $2 75; Sheep, $3 00; Half Calf, $4 75.

Thompson's Christian Theism: The Testimony of Reason and Revelation to the Existence of the Supreme Being. (The First Burnett Prize of $9000 was awarded to this Treatise.) 12mo, Muslin, $1 25; Half Calf, $2 10.

Thomson's Land and the Book; or, Biblical Illustrations drawn from the Manners and Customs, the Scenes and the Scenery of the Holy Land. With two elaborate Maps of Palestine, an Accurate Plan of Jerusalem, and *several Hundred Engravings*, representing the Scenery, Topography, and Productions of the Holy Land, and the Costumes, Manners, and Habits of the People. Two elegant Large 12mo Volumes, Muslin, $3 50; Half Calf, $5 20; Half Calf extra, $5 50; Half Morocco extra, $6 00.

Ticknor's History of Spanish Literature. 3 vols. 8vo, Muslin, $6 00; Sheep extra, $6 75; Half Calf, $9 00.

Vaux's Villas and Cottages: A Series of Designs prepared for Execution in the United States. Illustrated by 300 Engravings. 8vo, Muslin, $2 00; Half Calf, $3 00.

Wharton's Queens of Society. Illustrations. Large 12mo, Muslin, $1 50.

Wharton's Wits and Beaux of Society. Illustrations. Large 12mo, Muslin, $1 50.

Wilkinson's Ancient Egyptians. Illustrated with 500 Wood-cuts. 2 vols. 12mo, Muslin, $2 00; Half Calf, $3 70.

Harper's Catalogue.

A New Descriptive Catalogue of Harper & Brothers' Publications is now ready for distribution, and may be obtained gratuitously on application to the Publishers personally, or by letter inclosing Six Cents in postage stamps. The attention of gentlemen, in town or country, designing to form Libraries or enrich their literary collections, is respectfully invited to this Catalogue, which will be found to comprise a large proportion of the standard and most esteemed works in English Literature—comprehending more than two thousand volumes—which are offered, in most instances, at less than one half the cost of similar productions in England. To Librarians and others connected with Schools, Colleges, &c., who may not have access to a reliable guide in forming the true estimate of literary productions, it is believed this Catalogue will prove especially valuable as a manual of reference. To prevent disappointment, it is suggested that, whenever books can not be obtained through any bookseller or local agent, applications with remittance should be addressed direct to the Publishers, which will meet with prompt attention.

www.ingramcontent.com/pod-product-compliance
Lightning Source LLC
LaVergne TN
LVHW010227110826
845151LV00004B/1207
* 9 7 8 1 4 2 5 5 2 7 7 9 2 *